CW00693639

OFFICIAL

Cambridge English

EXAM BOOSTER

WITH ANSWER KEY

FOR PRELIMINARY AND PRELIMINARY FOR SCHOOLS

Photocopiable exam resources for teachers

Helen Chilton and Sheila Dignen

Cambridge University Press
www.cambridge.org/elt

Cambridge English Language Assessment
www.cambridgeenglish.org

Information on this title: www.cambridge.org/9781316648445

20 19 18 17 16 15 14 13 12 11 10 9 8 7 6 5 4 3 2

Printed in the United Kingdom by Latimer Trend

A catalogue record for this publication is available from the British Library

ISBN 978-1-316-64844-5

Additional resources for this publication at www.cambridge.org/preliminarybooster

CONTENTS

Map of the book — 4

How to use the Exam Booster — 6

Exam overview — 8

The Cambridge Scale of English — 10

Worksheets

Reading Part 1 — 12

Reading Part 2 — 18

Reading Part 3 — 24

Reading Part 4 — 30

Reading Part 5 — 36

Writing Part 1 — 42

Writing Part 2 — 48

Writing Part 3 — 54

Listening Part 1 — 60

Listening Part 2 — 66

Listening Part 3 — 72

Listening Part 4 — 78

Speaking Part 1 — 84

Speaking Part 2 — 90

Speaking Parts 3 and 4 — 96

Think about it — 102

Preliminary topic lists — 110

Answer key — 118

MAP OF THE BOOK

Paper 1: Reading and Writing 1 hour 30 minutes	Worksheet 1	Worksheet 2	Worksheet 3
Reading Part 1 p12 3-option multiple choice 5 questions 5 marks	**Daily life** Present simple and present continuous Making questions	**Social interaction** Phrasal verbs (arrangements) Making arrangements	**Hobbies and leisure** Talking about leisure activities Structuring a discussion
Reading Part 2 p18 Matching 5 questions 5 marks	**Health, medicine and exercise** Health vocabulary Opinions and advice	**Free time** Talking about free time activities Present perfect and past simple	**Travel and holidays** Holiday advice Present and past tenses
Reading Part 3 p24 True/false 10 questions 10 marks	**Education** Word order Collocations	**Shopping and services** Places in town Phrasal verbs (shopping)	**The natural world** Animals Word order of adjectives
Reading Part 4 p30 4-option multiple choice 5 questions 5 marks	**Places and buildings** Types of building Asking for and giving directions	**Environment** Environment vocabulary *Will* and *going* to	**Sport** Adjectives + preposition Sports definitions
Reading Part 5 p36 4-option multiple-choice cloze 10 questions 10 marks	**Entertainment and media** Short reviews Writing a biography	**Transport** Travel definitions Future forms review	**Weather** Extreme weather and environments Conditionals
Writing Part 1 p42 Sentence transformations 5 questions 5 marks	**Shopping and services** Reported speech Clothes vocabulary	**People** Reported questions Adjectives to describe people	**Weather** Strong adjectives and descriptive verbs Conjunctions
Writing Part 2 p48 Short communicative message (35–45 words, postcard, email, note, etc.) 1 question 5 marks	**Free time** Media vocabulary Reasons for writing Linking words	**Food and drink** Food preparation words Articles, countable and uncountable quantifiers	**Travel and holidays** Time expressions Phrasal verbs (travel)
Writing Part 3 p54 Longer continuous writing (100 words, letter or story) 1 question 20 marks	**Relationships** Relationships vocabulary Writing a letter or email	**Entertainment and media** Features of a story Narrative tenses	**House and home** Home vocabulary Structuring your writing

Paper 2: Listening 30 minutes	Worksheet 1	Worksheet 2	Worksheet 3
Listening Part 1 p60 3-option multiple choice 7 questions 7 marks	**Sport** *do*, *go* and *play* Comparatives and superlatives	**Travel and holidays** Airport vocabulary Making comparisons	**The natural world** Landscape vocabulary Adverbs
Listening Part 2 p66 3-option multiple choice 6 questions 6 marks	**Personal feelings** Adjectives *-ing* or *-ed*	**Daily life** *Used to* and past simple Past and present routines	**City life** Compound nouns Prefixes and suffixes
Listening Part 3 p72 Gap-fill 6 questions 6 marks	**Free time** Mixed-tense questions Offers and promises	**Shopping and services** Shopping vocabulary *have/get something done*	**Health, medicine and exercise** Parts of the body *-ing* and *to* + infinitive
Listening Part 4 p78 Correct/incorrect 6 questions 6 marks	**Environment** Present and past passive Easily confused words	**Social media** Social media vocabulary Conjunctions	**Language** Countries and languages Relative pronouns

Paper 3: Speaking 10–12 minutes	Worksheet 1	Worksheet 2	Worksheet 3
Speaking Part 1 p84 Examiner asks questions 2–3 minutes	**Daily life** Talking about you Family vocabulary	**Work and education** Job skills vocabulary Modals of ability	**Hobbies and leisure** Likes, dislikes and preferences Informal linking phrases
Speaking Part 2 p90 Discussion task with picture 2–3 minutes	**Shopping** Cause, effect and purpose *Make* and *let*	**Food and drink** Asking for and making suggestions Ordering a meal	**Free time** Discussing opinions *So*, *such*, *too* and *enough*
Speaking Parts 3 and 4 p96 Describe a photo 3 minutes (Part 3) General conversation 3 minutes (Part 4)	**Transport** Prepositions of place Managing a conversation	**Travel and holidays** Guessing information Expressing interest	**House and home** Home vocabulary Paraphrasing

Think about it p102

Cambridge English: Preliminary and Preliminary for Schools topic lists p110

Answer key p118

Go to http://www.cambridgeenglish.org/exams/general-english-and-for-schools/ for useful information about preparing for the *Cambridge English: Preliminary* and *Cambridge English: Preliminary for Schools* exams.

HOW TO USE THE EXAM BOOSTER

Welcome to the Cambridge English  EXAM BOOSTER

What is the Exam Booster?

The Exam Booster provides focused exam practice of all parts of the *Cambridge English: Preliminary (PET)* and *Cambridge English: Preliminary (PET) for Schools* exam. Prepare your students for the exam, ensuring they gain the confidence, skills and knowledge they need for exam day.

How can I use it?

- Pick and choose the areas you want to practise at any time
- Use alongside a coursebook or on its own; in class or for homework
- Photocopy worksheets for ease of use
- Use it flexibly to best support your students

How is it structured?

The Exam Booster contains 15 sections which follow the order of the exam: Reading Parts 1-5, Writing Parts 1-3, Listening Parts 1-4 and finally Speaking Parts 1-4.

Check exam paper, exam part and worksheet number at the top of each section.

Cover a variety of topics from the exam. Topics are suitable for both *Cambridge English: Preliminary* and *Cambridge English: Preliminary for Schools* preparation.

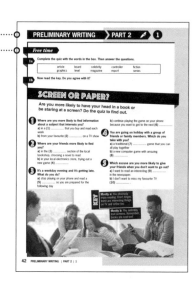

Go to www.cambridge.org/preliminarybooster to download the audio to your computer or device.

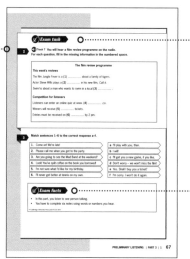

Find exam tasks easily. There are three worksheets for each exam part.

Exam facts offer clear, concise information about the exercise type and number of questions.

What other features are there?

Practise vocabulary, grammar or functional language tested in the exam using the additional tasks on the worksheet.

Exam tips provide practical strategies and advice on how to approach the task.

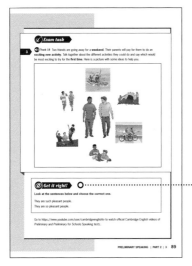

Help your students avoid the most typical mistakes that candidates make with *Get it right!* Identify and correct common errors made by real *Cambridge English: Preliminary* and *Cambridge English: Preliminary for Schools* exam candidates.

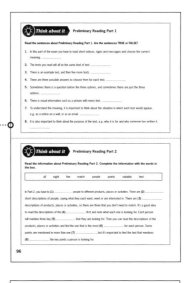

Use *Think about it* sections to check students understand what they need to do for each part of the exam – great either before or after attempting an exercise.

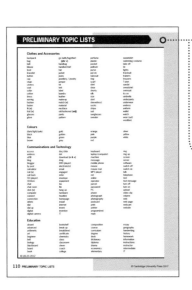

Learn and revise from the official Preliminary topic list.

Access a complete Answer key and Audioscript.

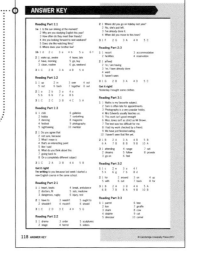

© Cambridge University Press 2017

Paper 1: Reading and Writing tasks

1 hour 30 mins

Reading

Part	Number of questions	Number of marks	Task type	What do candidates have to do?
1	5	5	3-option multiple choice	**Read five real-world notices**, messages and other short texts for the main message.
2	5	5	Matching	**Match five descriptions** of people to eight short texts on a particular topic, showing detailed comprehension.
3	10	10	True/false	**Scan a longer factual text** for specific information.
4	5	5	4-option multiple choice	**Read a longer text** for detailed comprehension, gist, inference and global meaning; as well as writer's attitude, opinion and purpose.
5	10	10	4-option multiple choice cloze	**Read a factual or narrative text** and choose the correct vocabulary and grammatical items to complete gaps.
Total	35	35 (weighted to 25)		

Writing

Part	Number of questions	Number of marks	Task type	What do candidates have to do?
1	5	5	Sentence transformations	**Complete sentences** to rewrite five original sentences so that the meaning is the same, but a different structural pattern is used. They must use no more than three words to complete their sentences.
2	1	5	Short communicative message, e.g. postcard, email, note etc.	**Write between 35 and 45 words**, communicating three content points given in the task.
3	1	20 (weighted to 15)	Choice between an informal letter or a story	**Write about 100 words**, answering the question of their choosing. Candidates are assessed using four subscales: Content, Communicative Achievement, Organisation and Language.
Total	7	25		

Paper 2: Listening tasks

about 30 mins
(plus 6 minutes to transfer answers)

Listening

Part	Number of questions	Number of marks	Task type	What do candidates have to do?
1	7	7	3-option multiple choice	**Identify key information in seven short monologues or dialogues** and choose the correct visual.
2	6	6	3-option multiple choice	**Listen to a monologue or interview** for specific information and detailed meaning.
3	6	6	Gap-fill	**Listen to a monologue and complete gaps** in a page of notes.
4	6	6	Correct/incorrect	**Listen to an informal dialogue** for detailed meaning and to identify attitudes and opinions.
Total	25	25		

Paper 3: Speaking tasks

10–12 mins

Speaking

Part	Timing	Interaction	Task type	What do candidates have to do?
1	2–3 minutes	Examiner ↓ Candidate	Interlocutor asks questions to each candidate in turn	**Respond to questions**, giving factual or personal information.
2	2–3 minutes	Candidate ↑↓ Candidate	Discussion task with visual stimulus	**Make and respond to suggestions**, discuss alternatives and negotiate agreement.
3	3 minutes	Candidate extended turn	Extended turn	**Describe one colour photograph**, talking for about 1 minute.
4	3 minutes	Candidate ↑↓ Candidate	General conversation	**Discuss** likes, dislikes, experiences, opinions, habits, etc.
Total		25 marks		

Cambridge English

The Cambridge English Scale explained

A guide to converting *Cambridge English: Preliminary* and *Preliminary for Schools* practice test scores to Cambridge English Scale scores

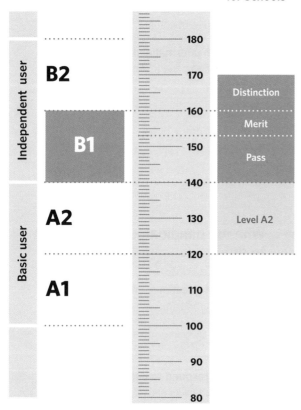

Cambridge English: Preliminary and Preliminary for Schools are now reporting results on the Cambridge English Scale. For these exams, candidates receive an individual score for each of the four skills – reading, writing, listening and speaking. In the live exams, each of the skills are equally weighted, and a candidate's overall score is calculated by adding all of the individual scores together and dividing by four (and then rounding to the nearest whole number). A candidate's grade and CEFR level are based on their performance across the whole test, and there is no requirement to achieve a minimum score in each paper.

The following tables can be used as guidance to help you convert practice test scores to Cambridge English Scale scores.

Please note that these only apply when using official Cambridge practice tests.

The conversion tables are intended to help you provide an indication of your students' readiness to take the relevant exam. The scores you provide may not always reflect the results the students may achieve in a Cambridge English live exam. They should not be used to try to predict precise scores in the live exam, but can be a useful diagnostic tool, indicating areas of relative strength and weakness.

The scores needed on any given test to achieve the scores on the Cambridge English Scale shown in the tables below will vary due to a number of factors, so borderline scores need to be reviewed carefully. The borderline is approximately three Cambridge English scale score points above and below the score needed to achieve the level, e.g. 137–143 for Level B1. Students who achieve only slightly higher than the Cambridge English Scale score for a given level on a practice test may not achieve that level in the live exam, and we recommend that they continue working to improve so that they reach the desired level.

CAMBRIDGE ENGLISH
Language Assessment
Part of the University of Cambridge

Cambridge English Preliminary

Cambridge English Preliminary *for Schools*

Reading

The Reading section consists of Parts 1–5 of the Reading and Writing paper. Correct answers in Parts 1–5 are worth 1 mark each. There are 35 possible marks in the Reading section.

Practice test score	Cambridge English Scale score	CEFR Level
32	160	Level B2
25	140	Level B1
15	120	Level A2
7	102*	-

*minimum score reported for *Preliminary*

Writing

The Writing section consists of Parts 6–8 of the Reading and Writing paper. Candidates' answers in the Writing paper are marked by trained examiners who are certificated to mark at the level. Correct answers in Part 6 are worth 1 mark each. Part 7 is marked using a short answer mark scheme and the total number of possible marks is 5. Part 8 is marked using assessment scales which are linked to the Common European Framework of Reference. 0–5 marks are given for each of the following criteria: Content; Communicative Achievement; Organisation; and Language. Whole marks only are awarded; there are no half marks given. Marks for each of the criteria are combined to give 20 possible marks for this part, weighted to 15. There are 25 possible marks for writing.

Practice test score	Cambridge English Scale score	CEFR Level
23	160	Level B2
17	140	Level B1
11	120	Level A2
6	102*	-

*minimum score reported for *Preliminary*

Listening

Correct answers in the Listening paper are worth 1 mark each. There are 25 possible marks in the Listening paper.

Practice test score	Cambridge English Scale score	CEFR Level
23	160	Level B2
18	140	Level B1
11	120	Level A2
5	102*	-

*minimum score reported for *Preliminary*

Speaking

Candidates take the test in pairs, but are assessed on their individual performance by trained examiners certificated to examine at the level. Candidate speaking performances are assessed using scales which are linked to the Common European Framework of Reference. The assessor gives 0–5 marks for each of the following criteria: Grammar and Vocabulary; Discourse Management; Pronunciation; and Interactive Communication. The interlocutor gives a mark of 0–5 for Global Achievement and this mark is doubled. Examiners may award half marks. Marks for all criteria are then combined, meaning there are 30 marks available in the Speaking test.

Practice test score	Cambridge English Scale score	CEFR Level
27	160	Level B2
18	140	Level B1
12	120	Level A2
7	102*	-

*minimum score reported for *Preliminary*

CAMBRIDGE ENGLISH
Language Assessment
Part of the University of Cambridge

Converting *Cambridge English: Preliminary* and *Preliminary for Schools* practice test scores to Cambridge English Scale scores

11

Daily life

1a Write questions. Use the present simple or present continuous.

1. the sun / shine / at the moment?

....

2. why / you / study / English / this year?

....

3. how often / they / meet / their friends?

....

4. you / look / forward / to / next weekend?

....

5. she / like / watching / films?

....

6. where / your brother / live?

....

1b Now match questions 1–6 in 1a to answers a–f.

a Yes, either at the cinema or at home. ☐

b Yes! I love Saturday and Sunday. ☐

c Because it's fun! ☐

d No, it's cold and wet! ☐

e Every weekend. ☐

f In London. ☐

2 Complete the quiz with the words in the box. Then answer the questions and read the results.

awake	buy	clean	go	go	have	late
leave	morning	routine	wake up	weekend		

Are you a creature of habit?

1. Do you need an alarm clock to help you .... in the morning?
a) No, I'm usually .... before my alarm goes off.
b) Yes. Without the alarm, I would just go on sleeping.

2. Do you always .... the same thing for breakfast?
a) Yes, I don't like making decisions in the .... !
b) No, that would be boring!

3. Do you ever forget to .... your teeth or brush your hair in the morning?
a) No, they are part of my morning .... , so I never forget.
b) Yes, if I'm in a hurry.

4. Do you .... home at the same time every day for work or college?
a) Yes, I don't like being ....
b) No, sometimes I'm early and sometimes I'm a bit late.

5. Do you .... shopping on the same day each week?
a) Yes, and I usually .... the same things each week.
b) No, it depends what I'm doing each week.

6. Do you usually .... to bed at the same time every night?
a) Yes, during the week, but not at the .... of course.
b) No, it depends what I'm doing each day.

Mostly a: You are definitely a creature of habit. You could try relaxing a bit and doing something different for a change.

Mostly b: Your habits and routines aren't completely fixed. It's great to have variety, but remember that routine can help you to be organised.

3

Look at the text in each question. What does it say? Choose the correct letter A, B or C.

1.

This week's fitness class will be half an hour earlier, at 6.30 pm, and in the sports hall, not the gym! Next week's class will be back in the gym at the usual time.

A The fitness class will only last for half an hour this week.

B There won't be a fitness class next week.

C The fitness class will be somewhere different this week.

2.

Tara, we've run out of coffee! Can you get some at the supermarket when you're coming back from college this afternoon? I'll pay you back tomorrow.
Daisy

What should Tara do?

A buy coffee tomorrow

B go shopping on her way home

C give Daisy some money to go to the supermarket

3.

BANK OPENING HOURS
Monday – Friday 9 am to 5 pm
Saturday 9 am to 11 am
The cash machine outside is
in use 24 hours

A You can't go into the bank on Saturday afternoons.

B The cash machine can only be used when the bank is open.

C The bank closes at the same time every day.

4.

Max,
There's a problem with the shower. You can't use it unless you want a cold one! Someone's coming to fix it this afternoon, so it'll be OK tomorrow.
Mum

A Someone is mending the shower at the moment.

B It isn't possible to have a hot shower this morning.

C Max will have to take a cold shower tomorrow.

5.

Hi Mia,
I might be late for the band practice tonight. I usually get the bus, but there are lots of delays this week. ☹ See you later.
Henry

Why has Henry written the text?

A to warn Mia that he may not be on time

B to remind Mia about delays on the buses

C to ask which bus he should get to band practice

✓ *Exam facts*

- In this part, you read five short texts – for example, signs, notices and messages.
- You have to choose the option (A, B or C) that means the same as the short text.

Social interaction

1 **Choose the correct words to complete the phrasal verbs.**

1. I usually meet *up / out / together* with my friends at the weekend.
2. I'm tired, so I think I'll stay *up / in / into* tonight.
3. Do you want to come *out / over / away* to my house later?
4. My family sometimes eat *out / up / away*. We like pizza restaurants.
5. Who does Max usually hang *up / in / out* with?
6. I was at a party last night and didn't get *back / out / to* until late.
7. We often get *in / out / together* to watch a DVD.
8. Do you fancy going *in / out / up* tonight, maybe to the cinema?

2 **Choose the best response.**

1. I've bought you a ticket for the concert on Saturday.
   - **a** Thank you. That's very kind of you.
   - **b** Yes, please. That would be lovely.

2. Shall I meet you at the station?
   - **a** It's opposite the bus stop.
   - **b** Yes, good idea.

3. Do you fancy going ice skating on Friday?
   - **a** I'm sorry, I can't. I'm doing something else.
   - **b** Yes, it was great.

4. I'm sorry I'm late.
   - **a** That's OK. No problem.
   - **b** We can wait a bit longer.

5. Why don't we go for a pizza later?
   - **a** No, I don't like it.
   - **b** Great idea!

6. Should I invite Emma to the party?
   - **a** Yes, I'd love to. Thanks.
   - **b** No way! No one gets on with her.

7. Is it OK if my sister comes to the cinema with us?
   - **a** Of course. That's fine.
   - **b** It doesn't matter.

8. Shall we meet up at the weekend?
   - **a** No, sorry, I don't want it.
   - **b** Yes, let's do that.

 **Exam task**

3

Look at the text in each question. What does it say? Choose the correct letter A, B or C.

1.

> ● ● ●   <u>Reply</u>   <u>Forward</u>
>
> Lily,
> Thanks for inviting me to your house next Saturday.
> I'm afraid I can't come because I'm going camping this
> weekend. Maybe we can meet up when I get back?
> Sara

Why has Sara sent an email?

A to accept Lily's invitation

B to ask Lily to go camping

C to make an apology to Lily

2.

Music festival
15 August
Music includes rock and hip hop
Tickets:
£6 in advance
£8 on the day

A There will only be two types of music at the festival.

B Some performances at the festival cost more than others.

C Tickets are cheaper if you buy them before the festival.

3.

> Hi Lucy, The football match
> starts at 5. I'm getting the
> bus to the stadium. I'll meet
> you there at 4.30. Don't
> forget to invite Sam too.
> Emma

What should Lucy do?

A get the bus to the football match with Emma

B ask Sam if he wants to come to the football match

C meet Emma and Sam at the stadium at 5 o'clock

4.

> You are invited to a
> **Jungle party** on **June 21** from **3 pm.**
> Dress up in an animal costume if you want to –
> a prize for the best one!
> Food and drink provided.

A Guests should bring some food and drink.

B Guests must dress up as a type of animal.

C Guests might win something if they wear a costume.

5.

> *Marcus*
> *Don't forget we're going to the cinema this afternoon with James. I'm not*
> *sure what film we're going to see, but we can decide when we get there.*
> *Jenna.*

Why has Jenna left a note for Marcus?

A to remind him about an arrangement

B to invite him to the cinema

C to suggest a film which they could see

☑ **Exam tips**

- Read each short text and think about where and when you might see it.
- Read the options carefully. Don't think an option is correct just because you see the same words in the text.
- The correct answer has the same meaning as the text, but usually uses different words.

Hobbies and leisure

1 Complete the speech bubbles with the words in the box.

club	dancing	festival	galleries	hobby	magazine
member	photography	sightseeing	sunbathing		

Anna I joined a chess **(1)** .... last year and I really enjoy it now. It's a great **(2)** .... because you have to really think about how to win. You also meet people.

Ilona I love **(3)** .... to great music. My ideal weekend is going to a music **(4)** .... and seeing lots of new bands.

Ben I love travel! My favourite activities are going **(5)** .... and visiting museums and art **(6)** ....

Lottie My ideal leisure activity is **(7)** .... on a beach and reading a fashion **(8)** .... So relaxing!

Karl I'm quite a creative person. I bought a camera last year and took up **(9)** .... I'm not interested in being a **(10)** .... of a club, though. I'm quite happy to spend time on my own.

2 Complete the dialogue with the phrases in the box.

do you agree that	going back to	like I said	not sure, because
on a completely different subject		that's an interesting point	
what do you think about this		what I mean is	

Sam: (1) .... museums should be free for people to visit?

Ellie: I'm **(2)** .... they cost a lot of money to run. It seems fair that people should pay something.

Sam: Yes, but museums shouldn't only be for rich people. **(3)** .... that everyone should be able to visit them, even if they don't have much money.

Ellie: Yes, **(4)** .... , and I agree with you in some ways. But **(5)** .... before, museums are expensive, and we can't expect the government to pay the full cost. **(6)** .... , Ana?

Ana: I'm not sure. I agree that someone has to pay to keep museums open, but **(7)** .... what Sam said, it doesn't seem fair that people who don't have much money can't see these wonderful objects.

Sam: Thank you, Ana. **(8)** .... , do you fancy watching a movie later?

Exam task

3

Look at the text in each question. What does it say? Choose the correct letter A, B or C.

1.

Hi George, I'm going camping next weekend, so can I borrow your tent? You bought one last summer, didn't you? If you've got a small cooker, that would be great, too. Thanks. Josh.

Why has Josh sent this message?

A to ask George to go camping with him next weekend

B to tell George about a new tent he's going to buy

C to ask if George will lend him some camping equipment

2.

●●●   Reply   Forward
To: Photography club members
Subject: Picnic

Everyone welcome – just meet at the park 2.30 on Saturday. Bring something for the barbecue – drinks provided. Bring your best pictures to share. See you there!
Tom

What should club members do?

A come to the picnic with food to cook

B take lots of photos at the picnic

C tell Tom if they want to go to the picnic

3.

Art workshop
Saturdays 10.30 – 12.30
From 15 September for 5 weeks
Suitable for all abilities

A There will be five workshops each week.

B You don't have to be talented to go to the workshops.

C The final workshop is on Saturday 15 September.

4.

If you enjoy playing the guitar and hanging out making music, contact us, Neil and Joe. No plans to play as a band - we just relax and play!
Call 07796 245798

Call this number if you want to

A play music with others

B learn the guitar

C join a band

5.

Stamp collection for sale
Over 12,000 stamps from a range of countries
Some antique and rare items
On offer as a collection only,
not as individual items

A The stamps are all very old.

B Some of the stamps are very unusual.

C You can buy just a few of the stamps.

 **Get it right!**

Look at the sentence below. Then try to correct the mistake.

I write to you because last week I started a new English course in the same school.

Health, medicine and exercise

1 Complete the statements with the words in the box.

ambulance	beats	break	dangerous	doctors	fit
heart	injury	medicine	rest	rugby	sick

1. If your .... is healthy, it usually .... around 70 times per minute.
2. According to .... , you should exercise for an hour a day to keep ....
3. Horse-riding is a more .... sport than .... or football.
4. If you .... your arm, you should call an .... to take you to hospital immediately.
5. If you feel .... after eating something, you should go to a pharmacy to get some ....
6. If an .... is painful, you should always .... the part of your body that's hurt.

2 Choose the correct modal verbs to complete the health advice.

1. I'm sorry, you can't see the doctor today. You *have to / mustn't* make an appointment.
2. You *don't have to / shouldn't* eat if you have stomach ache, but it's important to drink.
3. You *needn't / should* worry – it isn't a very serious operation.
4. It's important to rest. You *don't have to / mustn't* do anything for a few days.
5. I think you've got a fever. You *ought to / shouldn't* see a doctor.
6. You *don't have to / should* drink lots if you have a cold or a sore throat.

☑ Exam task

3 The people below all want to join a sports class. On the next page there are descriptions of eight classes. Decide which class would be the most suitable for the following people. For 1–5 write the correct letter A–H.

1. Chloe enjoys team sports but doesn't want to play in competitions. She needs a morning class. She doesn't have much money and can't afford to buy expensive equipment. ☐

2. Mike isn't very fit. He would like to get fitter, but he finds exercise boring. He's looking for an evening class that is different every week. He'd also like to see how he is improving over time. ☐

3. Sofia loves sport but is recovering from a serious injury. She wants to train in the afternoon with someone who understands her injury and can give her advice on exercises she can do at home. ☐

4. Jack is very fit and is planning a challenging 200 km run. He wants to train at least twice a week and would like some personal training too. He wants to train indoors and outdoors. ☐

5. Tara takes sport seriously. She plays hockey and tennis and wants to improve her skills and take part in competitions. She isn't free from Monday to Friday. ☐

Sports classes

A Sport for life

Weekly sessions in seven different sports, including squash, tennis and basketball. Do your favourite sport or try new ones each week. Classes take place on Thursdays 3–4 pm and Sundays 2–3.30 pm in Green Park and in the Park Gym. We don't believe in winners and losers, just having fun!

B Top training

Our club offers individual training sessions in the gym, with a personal trainer. The class is ideal for people who enjoy training alone and are keen to improve their fitness, or people who have particular difficulties with their fitness. Classes: every morning 9–11 am.

C Active plus!

This is a great class for people who enjoy playing sport with others in an informal way. Choose from a range of sports, including 5-a-side football and hockey. Classes are on Saturdays from 9–11 am. We provide balls, hockey sticks, etc. and a monthly report on how your fitness is improving.

D Water-cise!

Have fun and get fit at your local sports centre! Classes every Tuesday and Thursday from 6–8 pm. No two classes are the same! We organise regular competitions and also offer individual fitness checks every month, plus the chance to gain progress certificates.

E Fitness for All

If you're looking for a gentle, low-cost exercise class, Fitness for All offers exercises to improve your strength and confidence slowly. Our trainers are qualified to help with individual problems and can give you extra ideas to try outside the class. No equipment necessary. Classes: every Tuesday from 2–4 pm.

F Sport for all

This class is for people who want to take up a sport such as football or tennis for the first time. It's a great way to get fit in the fresh air. Classes start with training exercises, followed by a game or small tournament. Classes: every Tuesday and Thursday, 6–8 pm. All equipment provided.

G Rising stars

We believe sports are for winners! We offer training from professional sports coaches to help you become a more successful player. Choose from a range of team and racket sports. Players are encouraged to join local and national leagues. Classes: every Saturday and Sunday, or book an individual lesson with one of our trainers.

H Go for it!

This is a class for people who want to push themselves so they can compete against other people or themselves! Training takes place every Tuesday, Thursday and Saturday. Classes involve a one-hour run in the park, followed by weight training in the gym. Individual coaching and advice on improving fitness at home are also available.

☑ *Exam facts*

- In this part, you read descriptions of five people.
- You also read eight texts on the same topic.
- You have to match what each person requires to one of the eight texts.

© Cambridge University Press and UCLES 2015

Free time

1 Complete what the people say with the words in the box.

drama	horror	order	sculptures	stage	videos

Lily " I'm really into **(1)** .... , so I love being in plays. It feels great being up on the **(2)** .... in front of lots of people. I don't want to do it as a job, but it's fun to do in your free time! "

Jamie " I often organise a movie night at the weekend. I invite a few friends, and we **(3)** .... a takeaway. My favourite films are **(4)** .... movies, especially really scary ones! "

Rosie " I'm quite creative, so I do a lot of art classes in my free time. I don't like painting, but I love making **(5)** .... out of wood. I also make my own five-minute **(6)** .... , which I put online for friends to watch. "

2 Write the questions and answers. Use the present perfect or past simple.

1. **A:** where / you go / on holiday / last year? ....
    B: I went to Spain.

2. **A:** Is Martha still here?
    B: No, she / just / leave ....

3. **A:** Don't forget to order the tickets online.
    B: It's OK. I / already / do / it ....

4. **A:** when / you / move / to this town? ....
    B: It was about two years ago.

☑ Exam task

3 The people below all want to find a new free-time activity. On the next page there are descriptions of eight clubs. Decide which club would be the most suitable for the following people. For 1–5 write the correct letter A–H.

1. Emma loves using her imagination in a creative way. She loves working on projects with other people, and she would like to visit places and see creative people at work. ☐

2. Marco loves making things, and he enjoys meeting people from other cultures. He would like to learn a skill that he can use outside the class. ☐

3. Amina is interested in serious issues. She enjoys listening to talks and learning about life in other countries. She would also like to discuss her ideas and opinions with other people. ☐

4. Niko enjoys going to different places and meeting people from different backgrounds. He's also keen to find out about the place where he lives. He's especially interested in history. ☐

5. Erica is keen to help other people. She enjoys events where there are crowds of people. She wants to learn skills she can use in a job when she finishes her studies. ☐

Activity clubs

A Think!

Do you want to know more about international events? We meet once a week for an informal discussion. Each week we watch a film from around the world and/or invite speakers to help us understand recent events. At our next meeting we are showing a film about earthquake rescue teams.

B Games and chat

We meet once a week to play computer games. We give our views on new games and talk about games past and present. We also organise trips to game shows to see how designers come up with new ideas and create new games. You'll discover a whole new world!

C Party Plus

At Party Plus, we are looking for new people to help. We organise street parties and concerts to raise money for local charities. It's challenging work, and you have to work with a wide range of people, but you'll have a lot to offer future employers, and you'll make a difference!

D Come dine with me

We meet regularly to visit restaurants and enjoy eating delicious food from all over the world. We also invite chefs from other countries to tell us about how food is grown and prepared where they come from. There's usually quite a large group of us, so it's a wonderful way to meet people.

E Nature lovers

Are you interested in nature? Our group has been exploring the wildlife of the city for over 100 years! We organise talks from experts on the animals and plants around us. We also work in small groups to think of ways to improve life for the animals and people in our city!

F Action!

We are a film club, but we don't watch films – we make them! We're always looking for new people with interesting ideas. You will do activities in small groups, so it's a great way to learn new skills and make friends. We also organise regular trips to film studios to see how the professionals do things.

G A world of food

We can teach you to prepare delicious dishes! Our trainers come from five countries, and they love to share their recipes and the history of their cultures. This class will teach you how to create wonderful food in your own kitchen. You never know, you might decide to become a professional chef one day!

H City explorers

Get out and about with City explorers! We explore our own city and produce information guides so that visitors can enjoy it, too. We also produce maps of the city, past and present, showing how it's changed. We often get together with groups from other towns and cities to compare information and experiences.

☑ *Exam tips*

- Read the descriptions of the five people quickly and <u>underline</u> the most important information.
- The same information is often written using different words or phrases in the descriptions and the texts.
- Make sure the text you choose matches all the requirements in the person's description.

Travel and holidays

1 Complete the holiday advice with the words in the box.

accommodation	facilities	reservation	resort

I'm going on holiday to Turkey in two weeks and staying at the Bright Sands holiday **(1)** .... I haven't been before. Any advice?

- I went last year and loved it. It's got great **(2)** .... , especially the swimming pools!
- If you're expecting luxury **(3)** .... , you may be disappointed. But the rooms are all clean.
- If you booked online, check your **(4)** .... before you go. There was a problem with mine.

2 Complete the email with the correct form of the verbs in brackets. Use the present continuous, past simple or present perfect.

> ● ● ●   **Reply**   **Forward**
>
> Hi Beth,
> Joe and I **(1)** .... (arrive) in New York three days ago, and we
> **(2)** .... (have) a great time here. We **(3)** ....
> (already / do) quite a lot. Yesterday we **(4)** .... (go) up the Empire State
> Building – amazing. We **(5)** .... (not see) a show on Broadway yet, but
> we've got tickets for tomorrow!
> Abbie

☑ Exam task

3 The people below all want to go on holiday. On the next page there are descriptions of eight holidays. Decide which holiday would be the most suitable for the following people. For 1–5 write the correct letter A–H.

1. George wants a holiday with a big group of friends. They are into sports and want to do different things every day. He doesn't like boats, and some in the group have young children. ☐

2. Ana loves to be near the sea. She wants to visit different places, but she also wants to keep away from holiday resorts. She enjoys being active and learning new skills. ☐

3. Harry just wants to relax and have fun by the sea. He loves going out and wants to meet other people. He wants a cheap hotel and would prefer to pay for everything together. ☐

4. Jess wants to travel abroad and learn about a different way of life. She wants to stay with local people, not in hotels. She would also like to see some performances. ☐

5. Greg doesn't like crowded beaches and wants a peaceful holiday where there aren't many people. He enjoys walking in the countryside and is happy to spend some time alone with a good book. ☐

The best holidays

A Golden Sands Beach Club

There's lots to do at the Golden Sands Beach Club in Mallorca. It's a holiday you can afford. Enjoy wonderful beaches and swimming in the Mediterranean or take trips to nearby villages! Then enjoy shows and make friends at the social activities in the evening. All meals and drinks are included in the price!

B Making waves

Our learn-to-sail holiday in Greece will teach you all the basics of sailing. You'll be busy but will still have time to enjoy the silence of the open sea. We stop at a small harbour every night where you can enjoy local food in small restaurants, before sleeping on your boat. Price includes accommodation but not food.

C Forest Camp

Get away from it all at Welldale Forest. Stay on a local working farm or in cabins in the forest. Join in farm life or explore the many paths through the forest with our friendly guides. For those who prefer to relax, you can just enjoy time on your own listening to the sounds of the forest.

D Culture shock

Get away from the usual tourist destinations and visit India. On this tour, you'll visit seven cities, see the famous Taj Mahal and enjoy time at a beach resort. You'll stay with families and experience daily life with them. A full programme of cultural events includes some amazing dance shows!

E Seaview Hotel

Enjoy a week at this wonderful, small, luxury hotel in Spain. The price includes all food and drinks, and the facilities include a swimming pool, tennis courts and a restaurant. We organise trips to plays and concerts in the evenings. There's also a beach where you can sit quietly and relax or read!

F Hotel on the sea

Enjoy two weeks of luxury on this cruise around the Mediterranean visiting seven popular destinations. Relax in the sunshine by the ship's swimming pool. You won't get bored as there are cinemas, tennis courts and a theatre on board, plus plenty of social activities in the evening.

G Active fun

Looking for an active holiday? This wonderful busy holiday resort offers tennis, swimming, golf and lots more. There's something for everyone. Lessons are available so you can learn something new, whether you're 5 years old or 55! Fun for all the family! Price includes accommodation and breakfast.

H On foot

Do you love walking? Try this walking tour in the mountains of Italy. Each day, you will walk with an experienced guide as part of a group of walkers, then spend the night as guests of local people. It's a great way to see some beautiful countryside and make new friends.

 **Get it right!**

Look at the sentences below and choose the correct one.

Yesterday I've bought some clothes.
Yesterday I bought some clothes.

Education

1 Put the words into the correct order to make sentences.

1. favourite / maths / my / subject / is

Maths ....

2. often / Sam / for / appointments / late / is

Sam ....

3. hobby / photography / popular / is / very / a

Photography ....

4. Mrs / usually / us / teaches / Edwards

Mrs ....

5. work / this / enough / isn't / good

This ....!

6. Mr Brown / strict / as / Miss Jones / as / isn't

Miss Jones ....

7. too / test / the / for / was / difficult / me

The ....

8. work / checked / my / by / I / a friend / had

I ....

9. finished / we / eating / just / have

We ....

10. film / I / that / yet / seen / haven't

I ....

☑ *Exam task*

2 Look at the sentences below about an unusual school. Read the text on the next page to decide if each sentence is correct or incorrect.
If it is correct, choose A.
If it is not correct, choose B.

1. Ashton-on-Mersey School is very close to Manchester United's football ground.   **A B**

2. Young players join Manchester United from many different countries.   **A B**

3. Some young players start playing for the main team when they are 16 years old.   **A B**

4. Most young players go on to become professional footballers.   **A B**

5. Some football clubs allow their young players to stop studying.   **A B**

6. At Manchester United, young players have some experience of normal teenage life.   **A B**

7. Manchester United's young players have classes at school every day.   **A B**

8. The Manchester United students don't have to follow all the school rules.   **A B**

9. The main advantage for the school is that it receives money from the football club.   **A B**

10. One player helped some students to speak French better.   **A B**

Football stars at school

Can you imagine being a famous football star but still attending school every Monday morning as usual? That's what some students at Ashton-on-Mersey School in England do!

The school is about 7 km from Old Trafford, the famous sports stadium that is home to Manchester United Football Club. The club takes talented teenagers from all over the world. These young players come to the club to train. Even though teenage players are following their dreams of being sports stars, football clubs recognise that education should still be an important part of their lives. After all, only a small number of young players will go on to have successful professional careers in the sport, because only the best ones go on to join the main team. And although footballers can play professionally from the age of 16, most don't join professional teams until they are older.

All football clubs have to make sure players under 18 are getting an education, but many choose to do this by organising classes at the club. At Manchester United, however, young players go to a normal school where they can enjoy at least some parts of typical teenage life. That's why at Ashton-on-Mersey School you can see people who played against Arsenal or Liverpool on Saturday sitting down to classes with all the other students on Monday morning.

The Manchester United students have classes two days a week and study a range of different subjects. The rest of the week, they are busy training and preparing for games. But they still follow the rules like all the other students in the school. They are encouraged to feel part of the school, and they are also expected to set a good example to younger students.

There are many benefits to the school from their arrangement with Manchester United. The football club has given money to the school, which has helped it to provide a better education for all its students. Perhaps more importantly, seeing successful young players in the school can encourage younger students to try hard to do well and achieve their own dreams. There are also unexpected benefits sometimes, too. Successful players often return to visit the school to give talks to students. When one French-speaking player came back to visit, he was invited to join a French class for the day, and students were all keen to ask him questions! Chatting to an international football star really helped the students improve their language skills!

3 **Find the words in the text to complete the collocation for each definition.**

1. going to school .... school
2. do what they really want to do follow their ....
3. continue to have good football careers .... to have successful football careers
4. learn about lots of different subjects study a .... of different subjects
5. do what is required by the rules .... the rules
6. believe that they belong to the school .... part of the school
7. show other people how to behave .... a good example
8. give students better lessons and equipment .... a better education

☑ *Exam facts*

- In this part, you read a factual text.
- You have to decide if ten sentences about the text are correct or not correct.

Shopping and services

1 Match the descriptions to the places.

1. You can open an account here.	**a** charity shop
2. It's often outdoors and you can often find bargains here.	**b** post office
3. The money you spend here helps other people.	**c** bank
4. You go here to buy medicines and things for your health.	**d** department store
5. It might be self-service, or there might be a waiter.	**e** market
6. You go here to keep fit.	**f** chemist
7. You go here to send a parcel.	**g** sports centre
8. You can buy clothes and other things in this big shop.	**h** restaurant

2 Complete the sentences with the words in the box. One word is used more than once.

around	back	for	on	out	up	with

1. Excuse me, I'm looking .... the shoe department. Can you tell me where it is?
2. It's a good idea to shop .... and find the best price before you buy something.
3. That's a nice jacket – why don't you try it .... ?
4. The canteen used to be cheap, but they've put their prices .... recently.
5. I need a jumper to go .... my new trousers.
6. The shoes were so popular that they sold .... after two days.
7. If you don't like this jumper, you can take it .... and change it.
8. I haven't got enough money to pay .... all these things!

☑ Exam task

3 Look at the sentences below about a personal shopping service at Adlers' department store.
Read the text on the next page to decide if each sentence is correct or incorrect.
If it is correct, choose A.
If it is not correct, choose B.

1. Adlers' Department Store has just started offering a personal shopping service. A B
2. The personal shopping charge is refunded if you buy some clothes. A B
3. The personal shopper starts by showing you some clothes to find out what you are looking for. A B
4. Personal shoppers learn their skills from people who know the job well. A B
5. You should decide how much you can afford to spend before you come to your appointment. A B
6. You have to share a changing room with other shoppers. A B
7. A maximum of five people can attend an appointment together. A B
8. The personal shopper can help you to find clothes at reduced prices. A B
9. You have to book in advance to get an appointment with a personal shopper. A B
10. With the special offer this month, you can only save money on electronic goods. A B

Could a personal shopper help you?

Do you love shopping but can never find clothes that fit you or look nice? Or maybe you hate shopping and just want to get it done quickly? Well, why not come to Adlers' Department Store and try one of our personal shoppers?

Our personal shoppers have helped hundreds of customers over many years, both men and women. People of all ages have enjoyed the benefits of our service, and it doesn't have to be expensive. We charge a small amount for your appointment, but we give you this money back if you buy any of the items you try on.

Before you look at any clothes, our personal shopper will sit down with you and discuss what you are looking for – whether it's a special dress for a party, clothes you can wear to school or university, a smart suit for a job interview or just some new clothes to take on holiday. All our personal shoppers are trained in our stores by experienced staff to know what styles and colours will suit you best. It's a good idea to think about money in advance and set a limit on the amount you want to spend, so the personal shopper can find clothes within your price range.

Then comes the enjoyable part! You sit back and relax while your personal shopper looks at the huge choice of clothes in our store and selects items for you to try on. One advantage of having a personal shopper is that you get your own private changing room, so you can take your time, even if the rest of the store is crowded.

If you prefer to shop with your friends, there is also an option to have a group appointment. You can bring up to five friends with you, and you all get help with your shopping at the same time. It's great fun, and it works especially well if you're all going to a special event together. You can save money, too. When there's a sale on, your shopper can help you to avoid the crowds and find some amazing bargains.

If you're interested in trying our personal shopping experience, why not come along to one of our stores and talk to us? On days when the store is quiet, one of our personal shoppers might be free to help you there and then. But it's best to book in advance, to make sure you aren't disappointed.

For this month only, if you book an appointment with a personal shopper, we're offering a ten per cent discount on goods in all departments of our store, including electronic items such as computers and tablets.

So what are you waiting for? Get yourself a new look, and make shopping fun!

✓ Exam tips

- Read the whole text quickly before you answer the questions.
- The information in the text is in the same order as the questions.
- Underline the phrases in the text that tell you that your answers are right.

The natural world

1

Write the correct animal name for each definition.

bee	camel	cat	cow	dinosaur	dolphin	giraffe	lion	parrot	shark

1. a colourful bird that you can teach to talk ....
2. an African animal that hunts and kills other animals ....
3. a big fish with very large teeth ....
4. a friendly, intelligent animal that lives in the sea ....
5. a large animal that lived a long time ago ....
6. an insect that lives in large groups and makes honey ....
7. an animal with a very long neck ....
8. a farm animal that people keep for its milk ....
9. a small animal with soft fur that people keep as a pet ....
10. an animal used in the desert that doesn't have to drink very often ....

2

Complete the sentences with the adjectives in brackets in the correct order.

1. Lambs are .... animals. (farm, small, white)
2. Their dog is brown with .... spots. (black, round, small)
3. We saw some .... birds. (African, tiny, colourful)
4. Bears are .... animals. (shy, large, wild)
5. The puppy had .... fur. (brown, lovely, soft)
6. We saw a butterfly with .... wings. (shiny, small, blue)

☑ Exam task

3

Look at the sentences below about bees. Read the text on the next page to decide if each sentence is correct or incorrect.
If it is correct, choose A.
If it is not correct, choose B.

1. Lisa first saw the bees in her garden when she opened the window.   A   B
2. Lisa went back into the kitchen because she heard the bees.   A   B
3. Lisa was scared when she saw the bees.   A   B
4. The beekeeper thought it was funny that the bees had landed on Lisa's cake.   A   B
5. Even though the bees had eaten a lot of the cake, Lisa still ate it.   A   B
6. When John saw the insects, he knew immediately that they were bees.   A   B
7. John stopped his car because he wanted to call a beekeeper.   A   B
8. The queen bee was in the boot of John's car.   A   B
9. The bees followed the car because they could see the queen.   A   B
10. John got out of his car when the beekeeper arrived.   A   B

Bees, bees, bees

Most people enjoy seeing bees in gardens and parks, but it can be scary when they're flying together in large numbers, and it can be even more frightening if they come a bit too close!

A few years ago, Lisa Turnbull was in her home in York. She had made a cake and left it on the kitchen table. She was looking forward to eating it, but when she opened the kitchen window to help the cake cool more quickly, she unfortunately didn't notice the large number of bees flying around in her back garden. A few minutes later, Lisa heard a loud noise coming from her kitchen. She opened the door and saw a huge swarm of bees all over her kitchen table. The bees had left their old home and were looking for a new one. It seems that the queen bee, which controls all the others, had fancied a bit of cake and landed on it. She was followed by 15,000 others! Luckily, Lisa knew a bit about bees, so she knew they weren't dangerous and she didn't need to be afraid. She calmly closed the door and called a local beekeeper who found the situation very amusing and took the bees away. Although her cake wasn't badly damaged, Lisa didn't fancy eating it!

Last summer, John Norton from Manchester had a similar experience with a large number of bees. He was driving home after a long day at work when he noticed thousands of insects following his car. He realised after a while that they were bees and stopped his car, hoping that they would continue flying on and leave him in peace. However, when he stopped the car they landed on the back of it and stayed there. Feeling rather nervous, John used his phone to look online and find the phone number of a local beekeeper. John called him, and the beekeeper arrived half an hour later. It turned out that the queen bee had flown into the boot of the car while John was putting some shopping into it. When he closed the boot, she was stuck inside, so when he drove off, the rest of the bees followed. They somehow knew where their queen was even though they couldn't see her. John stayed in his car and didn't get out until the beekeeper had safely removed all the bees – which took over three hours! That's a good excuse for being late home!

 **Get it right!**

Look at the sentence below. Then try to correct the mistake.

I have just bought a new big lamp for my bedroom.

Places and buildings

1 Put the letters into the correct order to make words. Then match them to the definitions.

oiffce	psorin	hlostipa	ctotgae	fcatyor	gtues-hsoue

1. a room or building where people work at desks ....
2. a small hotel that is not very expensive ....
3. a building where people are sent if they have committed a crime ....
4. a building where people go if they are ill ....
5. a building where people make things, often using machines ....
6. a small attractive house in the country ....

2 Choose the correct words to complete the mini dialogues.

1. **A:** Excuse me, can you tell me **(1)** *the way to / how far for* the station?

   B: Yes, sure. **(2)** *Take / Turn* left at the traffic lights, and you'll see the station **(3)** *in front / by front* of you.

2. **A:** Excuse me, **(4)** *is it far / can you direct* to the museum?

   B: No. Just go **(5)** *straight off / straight on* for about half a kilometre, and the museum is **(6)** *on / at* your right.

☑ Exam task

3 Read the text and the questions below. For each question, choose the correct letter A, B, C or D.

A hotel under the sea

Want to sleep under the sea? The company Planet Ocean has plans for an exciting underwater hotel, which they hope to build in locations all over the world.

The hotel won't be large, with only 12 guest rooms, plus a restaurant. Guests will get to the hotel in a lift – so no diving or getting wet! The hotel will float 10 metres under the ocean, although it will be attached to the sea bed to prevent it from moving too far. Because it won't be very deep under the water, the sun will shine down and provide light. Guests will get great close-up views of the fish and other sea creatures, which won't be bothered by the hotel and so won't make any effort to avoid it.

The hotel's design, with walls made of clear plastic, means that when you are in your room, you will see the sea in front of you, behind you, above and below you. You will

almost get the feeling that you are swimming in the ocean. The luxury rooms will have excellent facilities, including a shower, TV and even the Internet. The restaurant will serve high quality meals. However, Planet Ocean want to encourage people to eat less fish, so you won't find any on the menu. The atmosphere will be completely silent though, so you will have to imagine the sound of the ocean around you.

The hotel won't be cheap to build, and it won't be cheap to stay in. But the designers are especially proud of the fact that it will be environmentally friendly. It will use electricity, of course, but it will produce its own, and won't disturb ocean life at all. In fact, the designers hope some sea creatures will build their homes on parts of the building, which will bring real benefits to the underwater world.

1. What is the writer doing in this text?
   A advertising a new kind of luxury hotel
   B warning people about environmental problems in the ocean
   C giving information about an underwater hotel
   D giving advice to travellers on which hotels to choose

2. What do we learn about the hotel?
   A Guests will have to swim down to get to it.
   B Its lights will shine into the sea so guests can see the fish.
   C It will only have a small number of rooms.
   D Fish and other sea creatures will be scared of it.

3. What can guests do in the hotel?
   A swim out into the ocean
   B watch the ocean life near the hotel
   C enjoy a meal of freshly caught fish
   D hear the ocean as they go to sleep

4. What is the best thing about the hotel, according to the designers?
   A It won't cost much to build.
   B It won't use much electricity.
   C It won't cause any damage to the environment.
   D Fish and other sea creatures won't come very close to it.

5. What might a guest in this hotel say?

   A
   > It's very expensive, but the facilities are quite basic and the windows are too small to see outside.

   B
   > It's great to stay in such a beautiful hotel that is also good for the planet.

   C
   > Seeing the fish up close is amazing, but it's a shame that the hotel disturbs sea life.

   D
   > It's a great idea, and I love the fact that it can move around and travel to different locations.

☑ Exam facts

- In this part, you read a text that includes feelings and opinions.
- You have to choose the correct answer (A, B, C or D) for five questions.

Environment

1

Complete the sentences with the words in the box.

bottle bank	climate	pollution	public transport	recycle	rubbish

1. I think that .... change is a really serious problem, and everyone needs to do more to prevent it.

2. I use .... such as buses and trains. I try to avoid driving because it causes air ....

3. I don't throw paper into the .... bin. I always .... it, to reduce the number of trees that are cut down.

4. I always take glass bottles to the .... It's important to use glass again.

 *Exam tips*

- The writer may be writing about their own experiences, or about someone or something else.
- The questions ask about the *writer's* feelings and opinions, not what *you* think.
- To find the answers to the first and last questions, you usually need to read in more than one place in the text.

☑ *Exam task*

2

Read the text and the questions below. For each question, choose the correct letter A, B, C or D.

The price of a perfect holiday?

Cruises are becoming more and more popular, with around 20 million passengers per year now enjoying holidays on board luxury ships. Many people see a cruise as the perfect way to sit back and do nothing, and enjoy time off work. But what is the effect on the environment of this trend?

Although it usually takes less energy for a vehicle to move through water than over land, cruise ships are often huge, with the biggest ones carrying up to 6,000 passengers. Moving such large vehicles requires enormous engines which burn as much as 300,000 litres of fuel a day. One scientist has calculated that cruise ships create as much pollution as 5 million cars going over the same distance. Because they are out at sea, they also burn dirtier fuel that isn't allowed on land. Unfortunately, no government has control over the amount of air pollution out at sea.

Cruises also produce huge amounts of rubbish, and cruise ships aren't usually good at recycling. Waste water from showers and toilets is usually poured directly into the sea – as much per day as from a small town. Waste food from restaurants isn't put into the sea, but still causes problems when brought back to the land.

Cruise ships also cause difficulties in the cities where they stop. Popular destinations can get five or six ships per day, with thousands of tourists at a time. Good for restaurants? No. Restaurant owners complain that the visitors look around for a few hours and then return to their ship to eat. What's more, the crowds can put off other tourists, who complain that the streets are too busy. Some towns have banned cruise ships or put a limit on the number that can stop at the same time. People who care about the environment worry that as the cruise industry continues to grow, so too will the issues for our planet.

1. The purpose of the text is to

   A persuade people that a cruise is a wonderful holiday.

   B criticise people who go on cruise ships.

   C explain some of the problems that cruise ships cause.

   D persuade governments to ban cruise ships.

2. One reason cruise ships cause a lot of air pollution is because

   A they carry large numbers of cars as well as passengers.

   B their engines are not as efficient as those of other ships.

   C it takes more energy to move through water than over land.

   D they use types of fuel that are not permitted on land.

3. What do we learn about the waste products on cruise ships?

   A All the waste products are carried back to shore.

   B Waste food is often thrown away at sea.

   C Most cruise ships recycle their waste products.

   D An enormous amount of the waste water isn't recycled.

4. Why are cruise ship passengers not popular in some cities?

   A They are sometimes rude to other tourists.

   B They don't spend money on meals.

   C They fill up the restaurants, so other tourists can't get in.

   D They complain when the city is too crowded.

5. Which best describes large cruise ships?

   A They seem to offer ideal relaxing holidays, but they aren't environmentally friendly.

   B They are becoming very popular, and they bring a lot of benefits, in spite of their problems.

   C They used to cause a lot of pollution, but things are improving now.

   D They cause pollution in the sea and on land, so cities are planning to ban them in the future.

---

3 Complete the sentences with the correct form of *will* or *be going to* and the verb in brackets.

1. Look at those dark clouds. It .... (rain).
2. I hope the concert .... (be) good tonight.
3. That ladder doesn't look very safe. I'm sure she .... (fall).
4. Why don't you borrow Jack's camera? I'm sure he .... (not mind).
5. I haven't done any revision. I just know that I .... (fail) my exam!
6. Are you going into town now? I .... (come) with you, if that's OK.

Sport

1 Choose the correct preposition to follow each adjective.

1. Netball is similar *with / of / to* basketball.
2. You should be ashamed *for / from / of* yourself for cheating in the game!
3. The city of Manchester is famous *of / for / from* its football teams.
4. We were very surprised *at / from / for* the result.
5. Are you interested *for / in / with* keeping fit?
6. Hurry up – I'm tired *of / from / with* waiting for you!
7. I'm not very keen *of / on / for* sport.
8. Who is responsible *for / with / about* organising the event?

 Exam task

2 Read the text and the questions below. For each question, choose the correct letter A, B, C or D.

Athletics in Jamaica

Jamaica has produced some of the world's best athletes, including stars such as Usain Bolt and Veronica Campbell-Brown. Is this success partly due to one event – the Annual Boys and Girls Championships?

The four-day Championships have taken place every year since 1910. Nearly 200 school students <u>take part</u> in front of an audience of over 30,000 people. The event is also shown on live TV, and the whole country watches what is sometimes called Jamaica's mini-Olympics. The <u>competitors</u> take it very seriously, and they all want to <u>win</u>. Classmates and former students also come to support and encourage their schools.

School <u>coach</u> Dwayne Simpson has <u>trained</u> many young stars. He believes the Championships have an important role in the development of young athletes. They are the biggest schools <u>competition</u> in the world, he

says, and other countries are now looking to copy them. He also believes that the Championships give young athletes a reason to practise. They want to do well for their school, so they work and train together as a <u>team</u>, so they produce better results.

Nathaniel Day, a young runner from Britain, has studied and trained in Jamaica for the last two years. 'Young athletes here get experience of being on TV from the age of 12,' he says, 'so when they're older, they aren't scared of big occasions and they perform well. In the UK, athletes don't perform in front of the cameras until they're adults, and sometimes they find it hard to deal with.' According to Nathaniel, the Championships also give young athletes a goal. 'Because it's such a big event, it gives them an idea of how exciting it is to perform in an Olympic <u>stadium</u>. It helps them develop the ambition to become champions.'

1. What is the writer doing in this text?

   A giving information about a famous Jamaican coach

   B describing the experience of taking part in an athletics competition

   C reporting an interview with a world-famous athlete

   D discussing the importance of an athletics championship

2. What does the text say about the Championships?

   A Thirty thousand people watch them on TV.

   B Young athletes take part just to have fun.

   C They started over 100 years ago.

   D Some former students take part.

3. What does Dwayne Simpson say about the Championships?

   A Other countries should try to hold a similar competition.

   B They have grown too big in recent years.

   C They encourage young athletes to do their best.

   D Schools are always keen to do well.

4. According to Nathaniel Day, the event

   A helps young athletes get used to being filmed.

   B is more exciting than the Olympics.

   C makes some young athletes feel nervous of big occasions.

   D is hard for some young competitors to deal with.

5. Which best describes the Jamaica Schools Championships?

   A
   It's an international competition which prepares young athletes for the Olympics.

   B
   It's an important event which helps young athletes to improve.

   C
   It's a huge social event which brings people together to have fun.

   D
   It's a local event which gives young athletes the chance to perform in a relaxed atmosphere.

---

3 Match the underlined words in the text on page 28 to the definitions.

1. a group of people who work, train or perform together ....

2. someone who teaches sports skills ....

3. an event where people compete against each other ....

4. join in with an event ....

5. be the best or get the best score in a game or contest ....

6. a large building where sports events take place ....

7. people who compete in a game or event ....

8. taught sports skills to people ....

⦿ Get it right!

Look at the sentences below and choose the correct one.

I'm sure that you will have a great holiday here.

I'm sure that you have a great holiday here.

Entertainment and media

1 Complete the reviews with the words in the box.

---
admission   audience   classical   comedy   exhibition
museum   orchestra   performed   plays

What's on this month?

Music in the Park

A concert of **(1)** .... music by Beethoven and Bach. It is **(2)** .... in Central Park

by the Berlin National **(3)** .... Brilliant!

Two's a crowd

A wonderfully funny **(4)** .... at the Royal Theatre. I saw it last night, and the **(5)** ....

loved it! It's written by James Garland, who has also written several very good, serious **(6)** ....

Animals in Art

A new **(7)** .... of animal paintings, which opens at the Victoria **(8)** .... next

Friday. Well worth a visit. **(9)** .... costs £3, but is free after 4 pm.

☑ Exam task

2 Read the text below and choose the correct word for each space. For each question, choose
the correct letter A, B, C or D.

Emma Watson

The actress Emma Watson grew up near Oxford in the south of England

and **(1)** .... as an actress at the Stagecoach School in Oxford.

(2) .... she had only acted in a few school plays, in 2001 she

was lucky enough to get the role of Hermione in the Harry Potter film

(3) .... This was the role which first **(4)** .... her

famous. She appeared in **(5)** .... eight of the Harry Potter films

from 2001 to 2011. After the Harry Potter films, Emma **(6)** .... to work in films, but

also **(7)** .... a few years studying English Literature at university. She acted while she

studied, and **(8)** .... 2012 she has continued to develop her career and has appeared in

(9) .... very successful films. She is **(10)** .... very interested in fashion, and has

worked as a fashion model for a well-known fashion magazine.

1. **A** trained   **B** coached   **C** taught   **D** learned

2. **A** But   **B** So   **C** Although   **D** Despite

3. **A** set   **B** series   **C** group   **D** collection

4. **A** produced   **B** made   **C** caused   **D** created

5. **A** each   **B** most   **C** every   **D** all

6. **A** continued   **B** kept   **C** stayed   **D** remained

7. **A** passed   **B** spent   **C** gave   **D** allowed

8. **A** later   **B** after   **C** past   **D** since

9. **A** several   **B** plenty   **C** lots   **D** few

10. **A** too   **B** besides   **C** also   **D** plus

3 Write a short profile of a celebrity. Use the text in exercise 2 as a model. Include

- where the person was born or grew up
- how their career started
- how they became famous
- their main achievements
- what they are doing now.

....

....

....

....

....

....

☑ Exam facts

- In this part, you read a short text with ten spaces in it.
- You have to choose the correct word (A, B, C or D) for each space.

Transport

1

Match the sentences to the transport words.

1. You sleep here when you travel on a cruise ship.	**a** return ticket
2. This big vehicle carries goods on roads.	**b** petrol station
3. You look through this when you are driving a car.	**c** cabin
4. This allows you to go to a place and back home again.	**d** hitchhike
5. You pay this when you travel on a bus or train.	**e** windscreen
6. You can travel like this if you don't want to pay.	**f** motorway
7. You buy fuel for your car here.	**g** lorry
8. You can drive very fast on this.	**h** fare

2

Choose the correct future verb forms in the speech bubbles.

1. Hurry up – our train *leaves / will leave* at 4.30, and we need to get to the station!

2. I've found a great hotel online. I *book / 'm going to book* it later today.

3. I *'ll travel / 'm travelling* to New York tomorrow – I can't wait!

4. Is your bag heavy? I *'ll carry / carry* it for you.

5. The prices *are probably going / will probably go* up, so I think it's better to book now.

6. The brochure looks amazing – I'm sure you *have / 're going to have* a wonderful holiday!

7. Boarding *starts / is starting* 45 minutes before the flight.

8. I must go and pack my suitcase – I *'m leaving / 'll leave* for the airport in two hours!

☑ Exam task

Read the text below and choose the correct word for each space. For each question, choose the correct letter A, B, C or D.

Travelling in the Glasgow area

The city of Glasgow has a modern underground rail network and **(1)** .... of buses and trains. It also has a **(2)** .... other forms of transport. The ferry across the river Clyde between Yoker **(3)** .... Renfrew is popular with tourists. There has been a ferry in service here **(4)** .... around 500 years. The **(5)** .... takes about half an hour, and it's an interesting way to see this part of the city. For a **(6)** .... boat ride, you could try one of the cruises on the Clyde. The cruises **(7)** .... at the Riverside Museum and sail down the river past some interesting historical parts of the city. If you **(8)** .... trying something more adventurous, you could travel from Glasgow to the island of Mull on a seaplane. The **(9)** .... are quite expensive, but it's an experience you won't forget. Also in the air, why not try a helicopter flight? It's not cheap, but you get an amazing **(10)** .... of the city.

1. **A** many   **B** enough   **C** plenty   **D** most
2. **A** few   **B** lot   **C** lots of   **D** a number
3. **A** for   **B** and   **C** to   **D** into
4. **A** since   **B** before   **C** until   **D** for
5. **A** trip   **B** travel   **C** transport   **D** route
6. **A** bigger   **B** longer   **C** taller   **D** higher
7. **A** leave   **B** depart   **C** start   **D** open
8. **A** fancy   **B** want   **C** hope   **D** plan
9. **A** costs   **B** fees   **C** fares   **D** charges
10. **A** scene   **B** scenery   **C** landscape   **D** view

☑ Exam tips

- Read through the whole text first.
- Look at the words before and after each space.
- Try each option (A, B, C and D) in the space and decide which is correct. If you are not sure, choose the one that sounds the best.

Weather

1 Complete the texts with the words in the box.

| dry | freezing | heat | humid | ice | lightning | showers | thunder |

Extreme weather facts

Antarctica is one of the coldest places on earth, with temperatures below **(1)** .... all year round. The ground is covered in thick **(2)** ...., but there is actually very little new snowfall each year.

Lake Maracaibo in Venezuela is known as one of the storm capitals of the world. You can see **(3)** .... in the sky and hear **(4)** .... on up to 250 days each year!

The Amazonian rainforest is one of the wettest places on earth. It is hot and **(7)** .... for most of the year, with frequent **(8)** .... or longer periods of rain.

The Lut Desert in Iran is one of the hottest places on earth. Very little grows in the extreme **(5)** .... It's also very **(6)** .... , with hardly any rain.

☑ Exam task

2 Read the text below and choose the correct word for each space. For each question, choose the correct letter A, B, C or D.

Weather forecasts

People have always tried to **(1)** .... the weather. In the past, people often watched the sky for

(2) .... of how the weather was changing. A red sky at night, for example, suggested that the

(3) .... day would be fine. Animals' behaviour also **(4)** .... information for

forecasting the weather. For example, if cows were lying down it meant it was **(5)** .... to

rain. Nowadays, **(6)** .... , scientists use complicated computer models to produce weather

forecasts that are much more **(7)** .... They can say, for example, if there is a 20% or 30%

(8) .... of rain on a particular day. They can also warn people if a storm is **(9)** ....

This is important for farmers and other people who work outside. It also helps ordinary people know

whether they need to **(10)** .... an umbrella with them when they go out!

1. **A** predict	**B** know	**C** tell	**D** say
2. **A** marks	**B** notices	**C** signs	**D** alarms
3. **A** last	**B** following	**C** later	**D** other
4. **A** sent	**B** shared	**C** allowed	**D** provided
5. **A** possible	**B** likely	**C** impossible	**D** able
6. **A** however	**B** although	**C** but	**D** despite
7. **A** accurate	**B** close	**C** true	**D** near
8. **A** luck	**B** chance	**C** opportunity	**D** result
9. **A** reaching	**B** getting	**C** going	**D** approaching
10. **A** bring	**B** fetch	**C** wear	**D** take

3 Complete the conditional sentences with the correct form of the verbs. Then decide whether each sentence is a zero, first or second conditional. Write *zero*, *first* or *second*.

1. If we .... (not have) a lot of rain here, the fields wouldn't be so green. ....

2. If lightning .... (hit) a building, it doesn't always damage it. ....

3. They will be OK on the mountain if the weather .... (stay) fine. ....

4. If you see lightning, you usually .... (hear) thunder soon after. ....

5. I .... (be) really scared if I found myself in the middle of a big storm. ....

6. If you don't get too close to the storm, you .... (not be) in danger. ....

7. We .... (go) to the beach if it's sunny. ....

8. I would love to take photos of a storm if I .... (have) a good camera. ....

 **Get it right!**

Look at the sentence below. Then try to correct the mistakes.

If I were you I will go to the countryside because it is a lovely place and it is very peaceful.

Shopping and services

1 Read what eight people said to Anna, a reporter, when she asked them for their opinions of a new shopping centre in the town. Then complete sentences 1–8 using reported speech.

1. Josh

> The big department store is brilliant!

2. Zoe

> I'm slowly starting to find my way around it.

3. Adam

> I've been there a few times, but I haven't bought anything yet.

4. Sara

> All the people my age will love the cinema!

5. Ben

> You can buy some amazing things there!

6. Eva

> It's great, but I spent too much money there!

7. Mark

> I never go to shopping centres!

8. Sofia

> Go and see it for yourself!

1. Josh said that .... brilliant.

2. Zoe said that .... way around it.

3. Adam said that .... a few times, but .... anything yet.

4. Sara said that .... the cinema.

5. Ben told .... some amazing things there.

6. Eva told .... great, but .... money there.

7. Mark explained that .... to shopping centres.

8. Sofia suggested .... and see it ....

☑ Exam facts

- In this part, there are five pairs of sentences.
- Part of the second sentence is missing.
- You have to complete the second sentence so that it means the same as the first one, using one to three words.

Exam task

2

Here are some sentences about a girl who likes shopping for clothes. For each question, complete the second sentence so that it means the same as the first. Use no more than three words.

1. Last week, someone sent Beth an advertisement for a new clothes website.

   Last week, Beth .... an advertisement for a new clothes website.

2. The website had a sale, so Beth bought a dress.

   There .... on the website, so Beth bought a dress.

3. The dress was too short for Beth.

   The dress wasn't .... for Beth.

4. The dress was less colourful than the picture on the website.

   The dress wasn't .... the picture on the website.

5. Her friend suggested asking for her money back.

   Her friend said, '.. ask for your money back.'

3

Match the definitions to the clothes words.

1.	They're a kind of jewellery.	**a** collar
2.	People wear this on the beach to go in the sea.	**b** belt
3.	You wear this under your other clothes.	**c** kit
4.	You wear these on your feet, especially in winter.	**d** earrings
5.	This is the part of a shirt that goes around your neck.	**e** underwear
6.	You might see these on dress or shirt material.	**f** raincoat
7.	These keep your hands warm.	**g** boots
8.	You might wear this if your trousers are too loose.	**h** swimsuit
9.	You might put this on in wet weather.	**i** gloves
10.	Footballers wear this to show which team they are playing for.	**j** stripes

People

1 Read the questions some fans asked their favourite celebrity, Jack Stark. Then complete sentences 1–8 using reported speech.

1. Ross

> Why are you in London?

2. Tara

> How long are you planning to stay here?

3. Daisy

> Can I take a photo with you?

4. Tom

> When is your next film coming out?

5. Emma

> Do you have any plans for the future?

6. Jack

> Did you enjoy filming in New Zealand?

7. Rosie

> Are you pleased with your latest film?

8. Jamie

> Will you move back to England one day?

1. Ross asked Jack why he .... London.

2. Tara wondered how long .... stay there.

3. Daisy asked if .... with him.

4. Tom wanted to .... coming out.

5. Emma wondered if .... the future.

6. Jack asked whether .... New Zealand.

7. Rosie asked whether .... latest film.

8. Jamie asked if .... England one day.

☑ Exam tips

- When you change direct speech into reported speech you often need to change the pronouns and the tense of the verb.
- Make sure the second sentence means the same as the first sentence.
- Don't write more than three words.

2

Here are some sentences about two brothers. For each question, complete the second sentence so that it means the same as the first. Use no more than three words.

1. I first met Chris and his brother Karl five years ago.

   I have known Chris and his brother Karl .... **years.**

2. Chris always wants to go out and meet new people.

   Chris is always .... **go out and meet new people.**

3. He really doesn't like to spend time alone.

   He can't .... **time alone.**

4. Karl is different to Chris.

   Karl isn't .... **as Chris.**

5. He isn't as sociable as his brother.

   He's .... **than his brother.**

3

Read what the people say about themselves. Choose the two words in the box that best describe each person. Use each word only once.

bossy	brave	cheerful	confident	generous	lazy
positive	relaxed	reliable	short	slim	smart

1. I'm not very tall, but I love being in charge and telling everyone else what to do!

   ....

2. Friends are really important to me. I'm never late when I meet them, and I love buying them presents, whether it's their birthday or not!

   ....

3. Everyone says I'm always smiling and happy. Maybe it's because I always try to see the best in situations.

   ....

4. I love wearing formal clothes, and I always try to look nice. I'm usually calm, and I never get stressed.

   ....

5. I hate working or doing sport! I'll do anything to avoid those things! Luckily, I'm not fat, though!

   ....

6. I'm not shy at all, and I'm not scared of things. I would definitely rescue my friends, even in a dangerous situation.

   ....

Weather

1 Choose the correct words to complete the sentences.

1. We had an awful holiday – the weather was *amazing / terrible!*
2. The strong winds *blew / moved* our fence down.
3. The snow usually starts to *fall / drop* in January.
4. It was a really *depressed / miserable* wet day!
5. My little sister is *anxious / terrified* of storms.
6. Let's go outside while the sun is *shining / lighting*.
7. We were all *brilliant / delighted* when the sun came out.
8. We've had a lot of rain – I hope the river won't *flow / flood*.

☑ Exam task

2 Here are some sentences about the weather in Spain. For each question, complete the second sentence so that it means the same as the first. Use no more than three words.

1. August is hotter than the other months of the year.

   August is .... month of the year.
2. My Spanish friend said, 'You shouldn't stay in the hot sun for too long.'

   My Spanish friend advised me .... stay in the hot sun for too long.
3. I prefer staying in the shade when it's very hot.

   I'd rather .... in the shade when it's very hot.
4. Most years, there is too little rain in the south of the country.

   Most years, there isn't .... in the south of the country.
5. The government encourages people to use water carefully.

   People .... to use water carefully by the government.

3 Choose the correct words to complete the text about the weather in Iceland.

(1) .... it is situated in the far north of Europe, Iceland's climate is not as cold as you might expect. The island (2) .... attracts a large number of tourists. From May to September, visitors can enjoy daylight almost 24 hours a day. (3) .... , it is often cloudy for at least a part of each day, so don't expect 24-hour sunshine! There are frequent showers, (4) .... , so it's a good idea to bring a raincoat with you. Winter is the time of long nights and colder weather. There are (5) .... frequent storms, which can be frightening. You might think this would stop the tourists from coming, (6) .... in fact the country is still a popular destination in winter, (7) .... of the bad weather. Visitors should bring warm clothing and a swimsuit (8) .... if they want to try a swim in one of the country's natural hot swimming pools such as the famous Blue Lagoon.

1. **A** However ☐   **B** But ☐   **C** Although ☐

2. **A** also ☐   **B** and ☐   **C** as well ☐

3. **A** Despite ☐   **B** However ☐   **C** Although ☐

4. **A** too ☐   **B** also ☐   **C** and ☐

5. **A** also ☐   **B** as well ☐   **C** too ☐

6. **A** and ☐   **B** but ☐   **C** however ☐

7. **A** despite ☐   **B** however ☐   **C** in spite ☐

8. **A** addition ☐   **B** also ☐   **C** as well ☐

◉ Get it right!

Look at the sentences below and choose the correct one.

My mom also said me to buy some T-shirts.
My mom also told me to buy some T-shirts.

Free time

1a Complete the quiz with the words in the box. Then answer the questions.

article	board	celebrity	controller	fiction
graphics	level	magazine	report	series

1b Now read the key. Do you agree with it?

SCREEN OR PAPER?

Are you more likely to have your head in a book or be staring at a screen? Do the quiz to find out.

① Where are you more likely to find information about a subject that interests you?
a) in a **(1)** .... that you buy and read each week
b) from your favourite **(2)** .... on a TV show

② Where are your friends more likely to find you?
a) in the **(3)** .... section of the local bookshop, choosing a novel to read
b) in your local electronics store, trying out a new game **(4)** ....

③ It's a weekday evening and it's getting late. What do you do?
a) stop playing on your phone and read a **(5)** .... so you are prepared for the following day

b) continue playing the game on your phone because you want to get to the next **(6)** ....

④ You are going on holiday with a group of friends or family members. Which do you take with you?
a) a traditional **(7)** .... game that you can all play together
b) a new computer game with amazing **(8)** ....

⑤ Which excuse are you more likely to give your friends when you don't want to go out?
a) I want to read an interesting **(9)** .... in the newspaper.
b) I don't want to miss my favourite TV **(10)** ....

KEY

Mostly a: You obviously enjoy reading. Don't forget, there are interesting things on TV and online too.

Mostly b: You definitely love screens. Remember, books are cool too!

2 Read the email. Find:

1. the sentence which says why Josh is writing ....
2. the phrase Josh uses to apologise ....
3. the sentence which explains why he can't come to the theatre ....
4. the sentence which suggests when and where they could meet ....
5. two linkers ....

●●●   <u>Reply</u>   <u>Forward</u>

Subject: Theatre

Hi Liam,
I'm emailing you about the trip to the theatre on Saturday. I'm afraid I can't go because I'm
going to visit my sister in London. Maybe you could come round to my house on Sunday
and we could watch a film together?
Josh

 **Exam task**

3 **You arranged to go to the cinema with your friend George on Friday evening, but now you aren't free. Write an email to George. In your email you should**

* apologise
* explain why you can't go to the cinema on Friday
* suggest another arrangement.

Write **35–45** words.

....
....
....
....

Exam facts

* In this part, you read a short text asking you for three pieces of information.
* The text may be a message or some notes.
* You have to write a short message of 35–45 words containing the three pieces of information.

© Cambridge University Press and UCLES 2015

Food and drink

1a   **Complete the two recipes with the words in the boxes.**

add	fresh	fry	onion	roll	serve	spicy	up

A

Cut **(1)** .... some meat and an **(2)** .... into very small pieces. You can do this in a food mixer if you have one. **(3)** .... salt and pepper, and some **(4)** .... herbs and form it into a round, flat shape. Grill this, or **(5)** .... it in hot oil. **(6)** .... it in a bread **(7)** .... , with tomato sauce or a hot, **(8)** .... barbecue sauce.

boil	butter	cook	cover	saucepan	smooth	stir	vegetables

B

Cut onions, carrots and other fresh **(1)** .... into small pieces. Put them into a large **(2)** .... with a small amount of **(3)** .... or oil. **(4)** .... slowly for a few minutes on a low heat, then **(5)** .... with hot water, increase the heat and **(6)** .... for about 45 minutes. Mix everything together in a food mixer until it is completely **(7)** .... **(8)** .... in a little fresh cream and pour into bowls. Serve with bread and butter.

1b   **Now match each recipe to a description of the dish. There are two descriptions you don't need.**

1. a lovely vegetable soup for a tasty winter lunch ....

2. a wonderful dish of meat cooked in a fresh tomato sauce ....

3. a tasty, healthy burger ....

4. a delicious pie made with meat and fresh vegetables ....

2

You went to a new café last weekend and you want to go there again with your friend, Jenna. Write a text message to Jenna. In your text message you should

- tell Jenna about the café you went to
- say what you enjoyed most about it
- invite Jenna to go there with you.

Write **35–45** words.

....

....

....

....

3

Choose the correct alternative to complete the sentences.

1. Would you like *a / some* biscuit with your coffee?
2. Stir in the chocolate, then bake *a / the* cake for 45 minutes.
3. I'm a vegetarian, so I don't eat *- / the* meat.
4. *- / The* French fries aren't very healthy.
5. I'm afraid I haven't got *any / some* orange juice.
6. There are *plenty of / much* dishes on the menu to choose from.
7. You don't need to add *much / many* salt.
8. I've got *any / some* fish for dinner.

 **Exam tips**

- Try to join short, simple sentences together using linking words like *so, because, as, despite* etc.
- Make sure you include all three pieces of information. In the instructions, <u>underline</u> the information that you need to include.
- You must start your message correctly (*Hi John, Dear Chris*), and include a suitable ending (*Best wishes, All the best*). Don't forget to put your name at the end of the message.

Travel and holidays

1 Choose the correct time expressions to complete the story.

I woke up early last Saturday morning. I was really excited because I was going to Florida to visit my uncle. I didn't want to forget anything! **(1)** *Then / First*, I packed my bags and checked the weight – no problem! **(2)** *Then / After* I made sure I had my tickets and passport. **(3)** *Before / Next*, I called a taxi to take me to the airport, and **(4)** *later five minutes / five minutes later*, it arrived. Everything was going

perfectly, but then we **(5)** *suddenly / sudden* hit a traffic jam on the road to the airport! **(6)** *In time / By the time* we got to the airport, I was really anxious. I hadn't flown on my own **(7)** *before / first*, and now I was really late. **(8)** *After / Later* I'd gone through the security checks, I only had ten minutes to get to the gate. **(9)** *Earlier / Finally*, I got onto the plane just in time, and was able to sit back and relax, and begin to enjoy my holiday!

☑ Exam task

2 **You have just got back from holiday. Write an email to your friend Tom. In your note you should**
* tell Tom where you have been
* tell him what you enjoyed about the holiday
* offer to show him your holiday photos.

Write **35–45** words.

....

....

....

....

3 Read the stories of unlucky travellers. Complete the phrasal verbs with the correct form of the words in the box. You can use the verbs more than once.

check	get	hold	put	set	take

When I arrived at the hotel, I got my passport out ready to **(1)** .... in at reception, but I found that it didn't exist – they were still building the hotel!

Last month, I **(2)** .... off booking my holiday for a few weeks because I was unsure of my plans. When I finally booked, they had **(3)** .... all the prices up!

I was travelling to Edinburgh by train last year. The train arrived at the platform and I **(4)** .... on. Unfortunately, I fell asleep, and when I finally **(5)** .... off, nine hours later, I was in Aberdeen – 200 km further north!

I was staying in a hotel last month. On the day I was leaving, I forgot to set my alarm and I **(6)** .... out 15 minutes after the normal departure time. They charged me for an extra day!

I was flying to New York last summer. The weather had been really nice for weeks, but on the day of my flight there was suddenly a big storm. My flight finally **(7)** .... off 16 hours late!

A few weeks ago, I was driving to Manchester to meet some old friends for lunch. I **(8)** .... off early, but I was **(9)** .... up in traffic for five hours, so I missed the lunch! Luckily, I still saw my friends!

◎ Get it right!

Look at the sentence below. Then try to correct the mistake.

He taught me much things which I didn't know before.

Relationships

1a Read about three problems with relationships. Complete the problems with the correct words.

annoying	arguments	ask	disagree	get on
in common	relationship	respect	share	similar

A

> I'm going camping with some friends this summer. I've got to share a tent with two other girls, but I really don't **(1)** .... with one of them. We don't have anything **(2)** ...., and I find her really **(3)** ....! What shall I do?
> Edith

B

I love my family, but my brother and I **(4)** .... about everything. We often have **(5)** .... and he doesn't **(6)** .... my opinions at all. I'd like to have a better **(7)** .... with him. What can I do?
Adam

C

There's a girl that I talk to at the bus stop every morning. We **(8)** .... a lot of interests, and I think we're quite **(9)** .... in a lot of ways. I'd like to **(10)** .... her out, but I'm scared she'll say no. What should I do?
Paul

1b Now complete the advice and match it to the correct problems.

getting angry	go out with	keep smiling	positive

1. Just go for it! She might not agree to .... you, but at least you tried! ☐

2. You can get on with anyone for a few days! Just .... and it will be fine! ☐

3. .... never helps. Concentrate on the .... parts of your relationship, and avoid topics that you don't agree on. ☐

2 On the next page, read part of an email that Emma receives and her reply. Find:

1. an informal phrase that Emma uses to start her email

2. the part of Emma's email that answers her friend's first question

3. the part that answers her friend's second question

4. three short forms that Emma uses to make her email informal

5. three adjectives and one intensifying adverb that Emma uses to make her writing interesting

6. an example of the present simple, present continuous, past simple, *will* and *would*

7. two phrases that Emma uses to make suggestions

8. three linking words that Emma uses

9. an informal phrase that Emma uses to end her email

I'm spending a year studying in Australia. It's great, but I'm really missing my friends back home. How can I make new friends here? How do you keep in contact with old friends?

Subject:

Hi Jodie,
I'm glad you're enjoying Australia. The weather in your photos looks absolutely amazing! I'm sure you'll soon make friends. You love sport, so why don't you join a sports club? That would be a great way to meet people. As soon as you get to know some people, you could organise a barbecue – that would be fun! I've got a few old friends from when I lived in London. We stay in contact online. We send messages and photos to each other, and we try to meet up when we can.
Take care and write soon!
Love,
Emma

 **Exam task**

3

This is part of an email you receive from an English friend.

We had a big family party last weekend, but it was awful. I argued with my dad, and my little sister was really annoying! Do you get on well with your family? How do you think I could improve things with my family?

Now write an email to your friend.
Write your **email** in about 100 words.

....
....
....
....
....
....

Exam facts

- In this part, you have to write either a letter or a story.
- You have to write about 100 words.

Entertainment and media

1 Read the story and answer the questions.

1. Which paragraph deals with the background to the main events?

2. Which paragraph includes the main events of the story?

3. Which paragraph includes a conclusion?

4. Underline two examples of the past continuous, and two examples of the past perfect.

5. Put boxes around three words that are used to order the events in a story.

6. Circle examples of adjectives and adverbs that make the story more interesting and exciting.

My day as a film actor

A

Last summer, a film company was making a film in my town. I had always wanted to be in a film, so I applied to be in a crowd scene. I was delighted when I was chosen!

B

The day of the filming arrived. First, they gave us our costumes. Next, someone did our make-up and hair.
I stood there nervously while I was waiting for my scene.
It had to be perfect! We practised 20 times. Finally, the director was happy and we filmed it.

C

Unfortunately, I didn't become a film star, but I met some famous actors and I had a fantastic day!
Three months later, I was very proud to watch the film that I had made!

2 Choose the correct verb forms to complete the sentences.

1. I didn't perform well because I *didn't learn / hadn't learned* all my words properly.

2. Daniel Radcliffe *played / had played* Harry in all the Harry Potter films.

3. She first *appeared / was appearing* on TV as an actor, and later she was given her own chat show.

4. I suddenly lost my voice while I *sang / was singing* on stage.

5. My sister went to drama school because she *had always wanted / was always wanting* to be an actor.

6. I met some famous singers when I was *working / had worked* at a music festival.

7. The star refused to answer when the interviewer *asked / was asking* him about his personal life.

8. A friend took me to see an exciting new band that they *were hearing / had heard* about.

3 **Your teacher has asked you to write a story.**
Your story must begin with this sentence.

I saw the advert for a talent show and decided to apply.

Write your **story** in about 100 words.

....

....

....

....

....

....

....

....

....

....

☑ **Exam tips**

- Writing a letter: make sure you include all the information requested in the instructions.
- Writing a story: make sure your story begins with the sentence given in the instructions and that it has a definite ending.
- Try to use a variety of tenses and structures in your writing.

House and home

1 Match the sentences to the house and home words.

1. You need to find this to get into a building.	**a** balcony
2. These look nice on your sofa.	**b** desk
3. Put one more on your bed if you are cold at night.	**c** cupboard
4. You can sit outside a building on this.	**d** entrance
5. Everyone has to do this, but most people hate it!	**e** roof
6. You keep your cups and plates in this.	**f** cushions
7. This is where you usually find the shower.	**g** housework
8. You can sit and work at this piece of furniture.	**h** blanket
9. Your rooms will get wet if there's a hole in this!	**i** stairs
10. You go up these to get to the first floor.	**j** bathroom

2 Look at the first line of a story in paragraph 1 below. Then look at the paragraph headings and write the sentences in the box in the correct order and in the correct paragraph.

As a result, I walked mud all over the carpet.
Luckily, I managed to clean up all the mess.
They came back after a lovely holiday.
They were on holiday in Portugal.
Then I decided to water their plants.
They never knew what problems I had had.
However, I spilled water all over the sofa.
Their flat always looked clean and beautiful.
First, I didn't take my shoes off before I went in.

Paragraph 1: Beginning of the story and background

1. *My friends asked me to look after their flat while they were away.*

2. ....

3. ....

Paragraph 2: Main events of the story

4. *Things soon started to go wrong.*

5. ....

6. ....

7. ....

8. ....

9. ....

Paragraph 3: What happened in the end / the conclusion

10. ....

11. ....

☑ **Exam task**

3

Your teacher has asked you to write a story.
This is the title for your story:

A new home

Write your **story** in about 100 words.

....

....

....

....

....

....

....

....

....

....

◎ **Get it right!**

Look at the sentences below and choose the correct one.

He said that he was interesting in visiting my house.

He said that he was interested in visiting my house.

Sport

1

Complete the sentences with the correct form of *do*, *go* or *play*.

1. Have you ever .... gymnastics?
2. I'm .... tennis with my friends on Saturday.
3. My sister .... horse-riding every weekend. She's the best rider I know.
4. I .... volleyball with friends last night. They're much better than me!
5. Do you .... yoga? I've heard it helps you to relax.
6. We .... swimming in the river last Sunday – it was great.
7. I .... a lot of athletics when I was young.
8. My friend Olly's .... skiing every weekend this winter.

☑ Exam task

2

 Track 1 **There are seven questions in this part. For each question choose the correct answer (A, B or C).**

1. What did the man do at the sports centre yesterday?

 A ☐   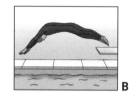 B ☐    C ☐

2. Which sport does the woman compete in?

 A ☐    B ☐    C ☐

3. Where will the friends go running this evening?

 A ☐    B ☐    C ☐

4. Which winter sport was Max good at when he was young?

 A ☐    B ☐    C ☐

5. What did the girl lose?

 A ☐
 B ☐
 C ☐

6. Which sports instructor is the man going to meet today?

 A ☐
 B ☐
 C ☐

7. What will open at the sports centre soon?

 A ☐
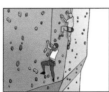 B ☐
 C ☐

3 **Complete the sentences with the comparative or superlative form of the word in brackets.**

1. My uncle's one of .... (strong) people I know.
2. That was .... (challenging) race I've ever competed in.
3. Oliver and Joe can kick the ball hard, but Dan can kick it .... (hard).
4. That was .... (exciting) match I've seen this year.
5. I find boxing .... (tiring) than ice skating, but I'm quite good at both.
6. This year, my coach has arranged a .... (reasonable) training plan than last year.

> ☑ **Exam facts**
>
> - In this part, you listen to seven conversations or monologues.
> - There are seven questions, each with three pictures.
> - You have to choose the picture (A, B or C) that matches what the people say.
>
> © Cambridge University Press and UCLES 2015

Travel and holidays

1 Complete the text with the words in the box.

boarding pass	check-in	customs	departure
destination	documents	luggage	security

When you arrive at the airport, you go to the **(1)** .... desk, where they weigh your **(2)** ....

and give you a **(3)** .... so that you can get on the plane. You have to show them your travel

(4) .... , such as a passport and airline ticket. Then you go through **(5)** .... , where your

bags are looked at, to make sure you are not carrying anything dangerous in them. After this, you go to

the **(6)** .... area, where you can have something to eat and drink while you wait for your plane.

When you land at your **(7)** .... , you have to go through **(8)** .... before you leave the

airport, where someone may check your bags to see what you are carrying.

☑ Exam task

2 🔊 Track 2 **There are seven questions in this part. For each question choose the correct answer (A, B or C).**

1. What time will the flight to Brussels leave?

A ☐

B ☐

C ☐

2. What does the man enjoy most about flying?

A ☐

B ☐

C ☐

3. Where will Maggie's family stay on holiday this year?

A ☐

B ☐

C ☐

4. What has the woman left behind?

 **A** ☐

 **B** ☐

 **C** ☐

5. What will the weather be like when the plane arrives?

 **A** ☐

 **B** ☐

 **C** ☐

6. What was damaged during the journey?

 **A** ☐

 **B** ☐

 **C** ☐

7. Where can you park your car for free?

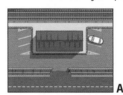 **A** ☐

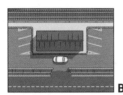 **B** ☐

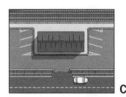 **C** ☐

3

Match 1–6 to a–f to make comparative sentences.

1. The train is not as	**a**	expensive hotels in it than that one.
2. Travelling by car is just as	**b**	late as it sometimes is.
3. This brochure has much more	**c**	is busier than I realised.
4. The tour guide was	**d**	boring as going by train.
5. Hong Kong	**e**	crowded than the towns.
6. The villages on the coast are less	**f**	more interesting than I expected.

☑ *Exam tips*

- Read the questions very carefully. <u>Underline</u> the most important words in the question.
- The people will talk about what you can see in all three pictures, but only one is correct.
- The first time you listen, choose your answers. The second time you listen, check that your answers are correct.

The natural world

1

Complete the words to match the definitions.

1. where a river drops from a high point to a low point w _ _ _ _ _ a _ _
2. the area of land next to the sea c _ _ _ t
3. a very large sea o _ e _ _
4. high rocks, often next to the sea c _ _ f _
5. a low area of land between hills with a river in it v _ _ _ _ y
6. there are seven of these large areas of land in the world c _ n _ _ _ _ _ _ _
7. a large forest in a very wet area r _ _ _ _ _ _ _ s _
8. a hole in the side of a hill or under the ground c _ _ _

2

Choose the correct adverb.

1. The rain fell so *heavily / angrily* on the roof that it kept me awake all night!
2. Snow falls so *softly / suddenly* that you can't hear it at all.
3. The sun shines *happily / beautifully* on the hills in the evening.
4. Ben shouted *strongly / loudly* to his friend who was lost in the fog.
5. The wind *lightly / kindly* moved the leaves on the trees.
6. The fox hid *curiously / quietly* in the cave all night.

☑ Exam task

3

◀》 Track 3 **There are seven questions in this part. For each question choose the correct answer (A, B or C).**

1. Which is the girl's favourite photo?

 A ☐  B ☐  C ☐

2. What should people **not** do?

 A ☐  B ☐  C ☐

3. What has the woman studied in college this week?

 A ☐   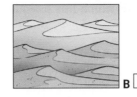 B ☐    C ☐

4. Where does the man prefer to swim?

 A ☐    B ☐    C ☐

5. What did the students enjoy learning about in the lecture today?

 A ☐    B ☐   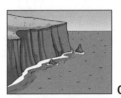 C ☐

6. How did the family travel in Iceland?

 A ☐    B ☐    C ☐

7. What did the friends learn about in the TV programme?

 A ☐    B ☐    C ☐

 **Get it right!**

Look at the sentence below. Then try to correct the mistake.

It's much more bigger than the old wardrobe.

Personal feelings

1a Match an adjective from A to the adjective from B which has a similar meaning.

A

annoyed	awful	challenging	funny	intelligent
miserable	nervous	relaxed	strange	surprised

B

amazed	amusing	angry	anxious	calm
clever	difficult	terrible	unhappy	unusual

1b Now complete the sentences below with the adjective(s) you think fits best.

1. I was really .... when Ted said he was getting married – I never expected that!
2. I find maths really .... I'm not very good at it!

  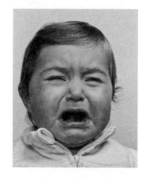 

☑ Exam task

2 🔊 Track 4 You will hear an interview with a TV actress called Brittany Briers. For each question, choose the correct answer, A, B or C.

1. Brittany realised that she really enjoyed acting when
   - A she played at being an actor at home.
   - B she attended some acting classes.
   - C she took part in a school play.

2. How did Brittany feel before her first theatre performance?
   - A worried about forgetting her lines
   - B anxious that she would use the wrong accent
   - C nervous about appearing in front of a large audience

3. Why did Brittany move into TV acting?

   A She needed to earn more.

   B She lost interest in theatre work.

   C She wanted to try something new.

4. What does Brittany still find difficult about screen acting?

   A having to repeat scenes

   B learning to speak more quietly

   C not having an audience

5. Brittany particularly enjoys

   A receiving a new part to learn.

   B attending special events for actors.

   C seeing her new films for the first time.

6. What does Brittany dislike about being an actor

   A not having many holidays

   B being recognised in the street

   C starting work early in the morning

3

Choose the correct adjective, *-ing* or *-ed*, to complete the sentences.

1. I found the talk on butterflies pretty *boring / bored*. I nearly fell asleep!

2. I'm really *confusing / confused* about what to do – can you help me make a decision?

3. Toni failed her driving test again – she was so *disappointing / disappointed*.

4. Wow! That film was *amazing / amazed*! It was better than I thought it would be.

5. Do you find science *interesting / interested*?

6. I'm so *exciting / excited* – we're going on holiday on Saturday!

☑ **Exam facts**

• In this part, you listen to one or two people talking.

• You have to choose the correct answer (A, B or C) for six questions.

Daily life

1 Complete the sentences with *used to* + infinitive, or the past simple of the verbs in brackets.

1. My sister Sarah usually goes for a run in the park after school, but yesterday she .... (go) swimming instead.
2. I .... (get up) very early every day when I was a kid.
3. My dad .... (work) for a large company but now he runs his own business.
4. I didn't .... (watch) the news, but I hate to miss it now.
5. The first thing I did when I .... (pass) my driving test was visit my friend in Scotland.
6. Supermarkets .... (close) on Sundays, but they're open all day now.

☑ Exam task

2 ◀))) Track 5 **You will hear an interview in which a businesswoman called Carla Smith is talking about her life and work. For each question, choose the correct answer, A, B or C.**

1. Why did Carla change the way she worked?
   - **A** She didn't enjoy the work she did.
   - **B** She spent very little time at home.
   - **C** She had health problems.

2. What does Carla say about running her own business?
   - **A** She continues to work a lot of hours.
   - **B** It allows her to take more holidays.
   - **C** She earns more than she used to.

3. What changes did Carla make to her exercise routine?
   - **A** She does more exercise than she used to.
   - **B** She does a new kind of exercise now.
   - **C** She exercises at a different time of day.

4. How does Carla feel about her health and eating habits?
   - **A** guilty about having too many snacks
   - **B** delighted that she has discovered new foods
   - **C** surprised that she now feels so much better

5. Where does Carla spend time with her sisters?
   - **A** in her own home
   - **B** at the cinema
   - **C** at the local pool

6. Which time-saving idea does Carla find efficient?
   - **A** checking emails on the way to work
   - **B** having a lot of similar clothes
   - **C** making lists of jobs to do

Put the words into the correct order to make sentences.

1. always / college / for / used to / late / I / be

    ....

2. Zijin / exercise / didn't / at / use to / all

    ....

3. son / teenager / as / my / a / get up / early / use to / didn't

    ....

4. eat / vegetables / Stephanie / used to / never

    ....

5. used to / reply / immediately / emails / you / to

    ....

6. coffee / a lot of / drink / used to / Ahmed

    ....

Now match sentences 1–6 in 3a to a–f below.

a ☐ but she's very healthy now.

b ☐ but he drinks more water now.

c ☐ but he's in a football team now.

d ☐ but you don't do it as often now.

e ☐ but I make sure I'm on time now.

f ☐ but he gets up at 4 am now!

 Exam tips

- Before you listen, read the questions and options carefully.
- The questions are in the order of the recording.
- Often you need to understand **when** something happened. Listen carefully to the words the speakers use – are they talking about the past, present or future?

City life

1

Test your knowledge! Complete the compound nouns.

1. There's usually a red one at the top and a green one at the bottom. Sometimes there's an orange one.
   t.................... l...................
2. This type of transport travels in dark tunnels.
   u................. t.................
3. This includes trains and buses. It's used a lot by people who don't have their own car.
   p................. t.................
4. You can find out about the attractions in the area you are visiting here.
   t................. i................. c.................
5. Lots of people in cities live in one of these. It has a lot of floors.
   a................. b.................
6. This is the middle of a very large town. It's where most of the shops and businesses are.
   c................. c.................

☑ Exam task

2

🔊 Track 6 **You will hear an interview with an architect called Scott Tenbury. For each question, choose the correct answer, A, B or C.**

1. What does Scott say about his 'capsule' apartment in Japan?
   - A It was too small for him to feel comfortable in.
   - B There was a lot of noise from nearby apartments.
   - C He had to think carefully about where to put things.

2. Scott says that the 'upside-down' house he lived in
   - A wasn't as exciting as he thought it would be.
   - B attracted a lot of interest from tourists.
   - C needed repairing regularly.

3. How did Scott feel when he had to leave his home in London?
   - A disappointed that it became so expensive to live in
   - B pleased to escape the effects of the weather
   - C amazed that so many people wanted to buy it

4. What does Scott enjoy about living in cities?
   - A having access to facilities
   - B getting interesting jobs
   - C seeing lots of people

5. What problem has Scott had with his 'water building'?

    A It's hard to find the right colour for it.
    B It's difficult to build on water.
    C It's not easy to get the right shape.

6. Why would Scott like to design a railway station?

    A to create something people love
    B to test his design skills
    C to improve transport services

3 ▶ **Add a prefix or suffix from the box to complete each word in the sentences.**

-ment	un-	dis-	-ship	-ful	im-	-ous	-ation

1. The Eiffel Tower is an ....forgettable monument. It's beautiful!
2. The subway near my house is a bit danger.......... . I never go there alone at night.
3. What a wonder........ square to live in!
4. I find it a bit of a ....advantage living so far away from work.
5. You live opposite that enormous depart........ store, don't you?
6. I live next to a big road. It's ....possible to sleep with all the traffic.
7. Excuse me. Could you give me some inform........ about bus times?
8. Friend........ is very important – everyone needs friends.

⊙ Get it right!

Look at the sentences below and choose the correct one.

I remember the beautiful beaches where we used to play volleyball.
I remember the beautiful beaches where we were playing volleyball.

Free time

1 Put the words into the correct order to make questions.
Then write your answers.

1. go / how / cinema / to / you / the / do / often / ?

....

....

What kind of films do you like to watch?

....

....

2. music / ever / you / festival / been / to / have / a / ?

....

....

What did you enjoy about it?

....

....

3. reading / you / do / enjoy / ?

....

....

What was the last book you read?

....

....

4. exercise / last / you / any / did / weekend / do / ?

....

....

Do you prefer to exercise alone or with other people?

....

....

5. play / musical / you / a / instrument / can / ?

....

....

Which instruments do you like the sound of?

....

....

6. gamer / a / you / are / ?

....

....

Why do you like gaming?

....

....

Exam task

2

🔊 Track 7 **You will hear a film review programme on the radio.**
For each question, fill in the missing information in the numbered space.

The film review programme

This week's reviews

The film *Jungle Fever* is a **(1)** .... about a family of tigers.

Actor Steve Wills plays a **(2)** .... in his new film, *Call it*.

Swim! is about a man who wants to swim in a local **(3)** ....

Competition for listeners

Listeners can enter an online quiz at www. **(4)** .... .co.

Winners will receive **(5)** .... tickets.

Entries must be received on **(6)** .... by 2 pm.

---

3 **Match sentences 1–6 to the correct response a–f.**

1. Come on! We're late!	a I'll play with you, then.
2. Please call me when you get to the party.	b I will!
3. Are you going to see the Mad Band at the weekend?	c I'll get you a new game, if you like.
4. Look! You've spilt coffee on the book you borrowed!	d Don't worry – we won't miss the film!
5. I'm not sure what I'd like for my birthday.	e Yes. Shall I buy you a ticket?
6. I'll never get better at tennis on my own.	f I'm sorry. I won't do it again.

Exam facts

- In this part, you listen to one person talking.
- You have to complete six notes using words or numbers you hear.

© Cambridge University Press and UCLES 2015

Shopping and services

1 Choose the correct alternatives. Then ask and answer with your partner.

1. How often do you *buy / spend* something new?
2. Do you enjoy looking at window *displays / shows* when you go shopping? Why? / Why not?
3. Would you rather *pay / spend* your money on clothes or on books and games?
4. Do you prefer shopping in department *markets / stores* or smaller shops? Why?
5. Do you like shopping *alone / yourself* or with friends and family? Why?
6. Do you enjoy buying *gifts / loans* for other people? What do you like about doing this?

2 Complete each sentence with *have* or *get* and the correct form of the verbs in the box. Use one verb twice.

cut	deliver	paint	repair	wash

1. I .... my hair .... about once a month, when it gets too long.
2. Hello, I'd like to .... my bike .... The wheel is broken.
3. My grandma .... all her shopping .... to her door now.
4. My parents have just .... the outside of their house .... white.
5. We .... the fence .... after it was damaged in the storm.
6. I never .... my car .... for me – I always do it myself.

☑ Exam task

3  Track 8 **You will hear part of a training session for people who are going to work as sales assistants in a large shop.**

For each question, fill in the missing information in the numbered space.

Training session for new sales assistants

The training manager is called Mandy **(1)** ....

New assistants will work on the **(2)** .... floor.

Part-time workers have a rest day on **(3)** .... every week.

Workers who live in the town can use the store's **(4)** .... service for free.

The staff discount cannot be used to buy **(5)** ....

Assistants need to collect their **(6)** .... on their first day.

☑ Exam tips

- You will hear different words or numbers that fit the space, but only one of them will be correct.
- Usually you only have to write one or two words in each space.
- You only need to write words you hear. You don't need to change them.

Health, medicine and exercise

1 Label the parts of the body.

1. ....
2. ....
3. ....
4. ....
5. ....
6. ....

☑ Exam task

2 ◀)) Track 9 You will hear a talk about an exercise class called Extreme Bootcamp.
For each question, fill in the missing information in the numbered space.

Extreme Bootcamp

The **(1)** .... use the name 'bootcamp' for soldiers' training.

Extreme Bootcamp takes place on a **(2)** .... so you can exercise and look at the river.

Members start each class at 6.30 am by doing some **(3)** ....

Wear the same clothes as for other exercise classes, and bring good **(4)** ....

The next bootcamp starts on **(5)** ....

Contact Ellie **(6)** .... for more information.

3a Complete the sentences with the correct form of the verb in brackets. Use *-ing* or *to* + infinitive.

1. Failing .... (take) your tablets on time could cause problems.

2. Many people avoid .... (visit) the dentist because they feel scared!

3. Can I suggest .... (see) the doctor about the headaches you're getting?

4. I'd recommend .... (rest) your ankle for the next week until it mends.

5. I'm hoping .... (get) the results of my X-ray this afternoon.

6. Did you manage .... (pick up) my prescription from the pharmacy?

3b What can people do to live a healthy life? Write a short paragraph with your ideas.

....

....

....

....

....

 *Get it right!*

Look at the sentences below and choose the correct one.

I will spend a few days to go shopping.
I will spend a few days going shopping.

Environment

1

Complete each sentence with the present or past simple passive form of the verb in brackets.

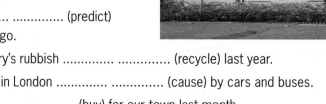

1. Waste plastic and metal ....
   (collect) once a week in our town.

2. Why .... litter never .... (pick up) in
   this park? It's always the same!

3. Climate change .... (predict)
   by scientists 40 years ago.

4. About 50% of our country's rubbish .... (recycle) last year.

5. Most of the air pollution in London .... (cause) by cars and buses.

6. Six electric buses .... (buy) for our town last month.

☑ Exam task

2

🔊 Track 10 **Look at the six sentences for this part. You will hear two local politicians, a man called Robin and a woman called Lisa, talking about recycling in their town. Decide if each sentence is correct or incorrect. If it is correct, put a tick (√) in the box under A for YES. If it is not correct, put a tick (√) in the box under B for NO.**

	A YES	B NO
1. Robin is surprised by how much recycling people do in his town.	☐	☐
2. Lisa thinks it takes too long to recycle metal.	☐	☐
3. Robin believes there should be more bottle banks.	☐	☐
4. Lisa thinks that people are making good progress with paper recycling.	☐	☐
5. Robin and Lisa agree that people need more information about plastic.	☐	☐
6. Robin thinks that people should pay less to use public transport.	☐	☐

Choose the correct verb to complete the sentences.

1. Could I *borrow / lend* your notes on the environment lecture we had today?
2. Does your family *do / make* much recycling?
3. I don't like *spending / wasting* water. I have showers instead of baths.
4. Will you *bring / take* those bottles to the bottle bank, please?
5. *Tell / Say* me what you know about safely getting rid of batteries.
6. I *knew / met* a scientist at the fair – she was really interesting.
7. We should *teach / learn* people more about recycling plastic.
8. Hurry up! We don't want to *lose / miss* the bus to the meeting at the town hall.

What can we do to help protect the environment? Write a paragraph with your ideas.

....

....

....

....

....

 **Exam facts**

- In this part, you listen to a conversation between two people that know each other.
- You have to read six sentences about the feelings and opinions of the speakers and decide if they are correct or not correct.

© Cambridge University Press and UCLES 2015

Social media

1 Complete the sentences and questions with the words in the box.

blog	chatting	download	podcasts	post	sharing	update	upload

1. When you 'talk' to someone online it's called ....
2. If you want to listen to music from the Internet, it's better if you .... it first.
3. Do you ever .... videos onto YouTube so other people can watch them?
4. How often do you .... on Twitter?
5. Do you .... your Facebook status every day so people know what you're doing?
6. Do you listen to .... on the Internet much?
7. I love .... funny videos online so everyone else can see them.
8. Have you ever written a regular daily or weekly .... about your life?

☑ Exam task

2 🔊 Track 11 **Look at the six sentences for this part. You will hear a young woman called Sylvia and a man called Ted talking about using social media. Decide if each sentence is correct or incorrect. If it is correct, put a tick (√) in the box under A for YES. If it is not correct, put a tick (√) in the box under B for NO.**

	A YES	B NO
1. Ted thinks he wastes time looking at Instagram.	☐	☐
2. Ted is surprised at how long Sylvia spends online every day.	☐	☐
3. Sylvia admits that she finds it difficult to sleep after looking at screens.	☐	☐
4. Ted and Sylvia agree that Snapchat is fun to use.	☐	☐
5. Sylvia thinks that some people use Facebook in the wrong way.	☐	☐
6. Ted and Sylvia both enjoying reading posts on Twitter.	☐	☐

Complete the sentences with *before, while, although, since, plus* **or** *unless.*

1. I spend hours reading online, ... I rarely remember what I've looked at!

2. I can browse the Internet for hours .... I realise how long I've been online.

3. Social media's a great way to keep in touch with friends – .... , you can make loads of new ones.

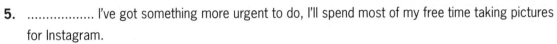

4. .... you know so much about uploading videos – could you show me how to do it?

5. .... I've got something more urgent to do, I'll spend most of my free time taking pictures for Instagram.

6. .... I like using social media, I think it's better to talk face to face.

What are your favourite social networking sites and why?

....

....

....

....

....

☑ **Exam tips**

- There is usually one female and one male speaker to help you understand who is talking.
- Usually, each question will ask you for the opinion of one of the speakers. Make sure you listen for the correct speaker's opinion.
- Sometimes the question will be about what the speakers both think. Make sure you listen to what both speakers say before you choose your answer.

Language

1 Complete the table with languages and countries.

Country	Language
Brazil	(1) P _ _ _ _ _ _ _ _
(2) S _ _ _ _	Spanish
China	Mandarin (3) C _ _ _ _ _ _
Turkey	(4) T _ _ _ _ _ _
(5) R _ _ _ _ _	Russian
France	(6) F _ _ _ _ _
(7) I _ _ _ _	Italian

☑ Exam task

2 🔊 Track 12 Look at the six sentences for this part. You will hear a man called Aaron and a woman called Sophia talking about learning languages. Decide if each sentence is correct or incorrect. If it is correct, put a tick (√) in the box under A for YES. If it is not correct, put a tick (√) in the box under B for NO.

		A YES	B NO
1.	Sophia thinks that Japanese is a difficult language to learn.	☐	☐
2.	Aaron and Sophia agree that it is important to learn languages.	☐	☐
3.	Aaron thinks he has a natural ability for remembering new words.	☐	☐
4.	Sophia feels worried when she can't understand what someone says.	☐	☐
5.	Aaron thinks writing is the most difficult skill.	☐	☐
6.	Both Aaron and Sophia think it is useful to make mistakes.	☐	☐

3 Are the relative pronouns in these sentences correct? Correct the ones which are wrong.

1. Finnish, Estonian and Hungarian are languages *whose* are not similar to any other in Europe. ....

2. People *who* live in India may speak one or more of its 22 official languages. ....

3. The translations *which* everyone did for homework were excellent – well done! ....

4. Language experts often try to record languages *that* are dying out. ....

5. *Whom* dictionary is this? You'll need it for our English lesson today. ....

6. People *which* can speak two languages very well are called 'bilingual'. ....

 **Get it right!**

Look at the sentence below. Then try to correct the mistake.

This party organised by my old school friend.

Daily life

1 **Write the questions and ask a partner.**

1. What | your name?

....

2. How | spell | your surname?

....

3. Where | you | come from?

....

4. Do | you | study English at college?

....

5. Where | you | live?

....

☑ Exam task

2a 🔊 **Track 13** Now complete the examiner's questions in Phase 2 of Part 1. Then listen and check.

1. Who do you .... most time with?

2. What do you .... doing when you're at home?

3. What do you .... about your school or job?

4. What .... you like to do in the future?

5. When did you .... learning English? Do you enjoy it? Why? / Why not?

6. Where did you .... up?

7. What do you like about the town you .... in?

8. Where would you like to live, if you .... the opportunity?

2b **In pairs, ask and answer the questions.**

3 **Complete the family words. Use the descriptions to help you.**

1. Your _ _ _ s _ _ is your aunt or uncle's son or daughter.

2. If you are _ _ _ _ _ _ d, it means you have a husband or wife.

3. Two people, such as a boyfriend and girlfriend, are known as a _ _ u _ _ _.

4. There are usually several g _ _ _ r _ t _ _ _ _ in one family: younger people and older ones.

5. An _ _ _ _ v _ _ s _ _ _ is the day on which an important event happened in a previous year.

6. Your _ _ p _ _ _ is the son of your brother or sister.

☑ **Exam facts**

- In this part, the examiner asks you questions about yourself.
- The questions are usually about your name, your daily routine, your likes and dislikes, where you study or work, etc.
- You only speak to the examiner. You don't speak to the other student.

Go to https://www.youtube.com/user/cambridgeenglishtv to watch official Cambridge English videos of *Preliminary* and *Preliminary for Schools* Speaking tests.

PRELIMINARY SPEAKING > PART 1   2

Work and education

1

Match 1–8 to a–h to make questions about job skills.

1. Do you have good	**a** organised person?
2. Are you a	**b** good at solving problems?
3. How well do you	**c** fast learner?
4. Are you an	**d** communication skills?
5. Do you enjoy	**e** at making decisions?
6. How good are you	**f** working in a team?
7. Do you generally have a	**g** manage your time?
8. Are you	**h** positive attitude?

☑ Exam task

2a

🔊 Track 14 Complete the examiner's questions from Part 1. Then listen and check.

1. Do you study or .... ? What are you studying? / What do you do?

2. Do you like your .... or job? Why? / Why not?

3. What is or was your .... subject at school? What do or did you like most about it?

4. Which .... would you like to learn more about?

5. What do you find .... about learning English?

6. How often do you use English .... of your English classes?

7. If you could have any .... , what would you do and why?

8. What is your greatest study or work .... ?

2b In pairs, ask and answer the questions.

3 Complete the sentences with the correct form of *can* or *be able to*.

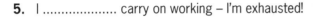

1. My daughter .... say the whole alphabet by the time she was three.

2. Which foreign languages .... you speak?

3. Do you think you .... finish the project by tomorrow evening?

4. Jenna has always .... get work, despite not having many qualifications.

5. I .... carry on working – I'm exhausted!

6. My brother .... count until he was six, but he's an accountant now.

☑ **Exam tips**

- The examiner will ask you to spell your surname. Make sure you know how to spell it in English.
- In phase 2 of Part 1, answer with more than one word and try to give examples or reasons for your answer.
- Listen carefully to the examiner's questions. If you don't understand something, ask them to repeat it.

Go to https://www.youtube.com/user/cambridgeenglishtv to watch official Cambridge English videos of *Preliminary* and *Preliminary for Schools* Speaking tests.

Hobbies and leisure

1a Match 1–6 to a–f to make sentences about hobbies.

1. I'm not keen on cycling because	**a** since the water's warmer.
2. I don't mind going to the gym, though	**b** it's cheaper than buying them!
3. I love making things because	**c** because they're fun.
4. I prefer team sports to individual ones	**d** it often rains where I live.
5. Although I'm not very good at it, I	**e** it's a bit boring.
6. I'd rather swim indoors than in a lake	**f** quite like dancing.

1b Now complete the sentences so that they are true for you.

1. I'd rather ....

2. I'm not keen on ....

3. I love ....

4. I don't mind ....

☑ Exam task

2a 🔊 Track 15 Complete the examiner's questions. Then listen and check.

1. What do you enjoy doing in your .... ?

2. Do you enjoy playing .... ? Which ones?

3. Do you prefer to watch sports rather than .... in them?

4. Do you enjoy .... things with other people?

5. What are the most popular sports or hobbies in your .... ?

6. What .... would you most like to try?

7. Have you ever tried any .... sports? Did you enjoy it?

8. How did you spend last .... ?

2b In pairs, ask and answer the questions.

3 Complete the text with *so, while, after, what's more, at first* and *anyway*.

Last week a friend of mine invited me to watch her doing her hobby. **(1)** .... , I was confused:

Why would she want me to do that? **(2)** .... , I went along to the local theatre, where a band

was playing that night. I arrived early, **(3)** .... I sat down and waited. **(4)** .... I was

sitting there, my friend appeared on stage with a huge piece of paper, which she stuck to a board. That

was strange enough, but **(5)** .... , when the band came on, she took out some paints and

brushes as well. As the band played, my friend painted to their music! **(6)** .... they finished

playing, my friend showed the picture to the audience. It was amazing!

 *Get it right!*

Look at the sentence below. Then try to correct the mistake.

But it would be better if you can take part, too.

Go to https://www.youtube.com/user/cambridgeenglishtv to watch official Cambridge English videos of
Preliminary and *Preliminary for Schools* Speaking tests.

Shopping

1 Complete the dialogue with the words in the box. There may be more than one correct answer for each space.

> as   because   could   don't   would   should   since   so

Sam: Let's make a shopping list for our barbecue party on Saturday.

Carly: OK. **I think we (1)** .... get sausages **(2)** .... everyone loves them!

Sam: Mm, but I **(3)** .... **think we should** buy too many burgers – there were a lot left after our last party.

Carly: True. We **(4)** .... get some fish **(5)** .... not everyone eats meat.

Sam: Yes, and **how about** getting some tasty vegetables?

Carly: That **(6)** .... **be a good idea**. And the children like chicken, **(7)** .... **let's** get some of that.

Sam: Great, and **(8)** .... your parents like jacket potatoes, **why don't we** cook some of those, as well?

Carly: Perfect!

2a Look at the words in bold in these sentences.

Let's buy Dad some new boots. Walking in the hills **makes** him feel relaxed!

Which word . . . ?

a   shows that something / someone causes another thing to happen

b   is used to make a suggestion

2b Now rewrite the sentences so they mean the same, using *Let's* or the correct form of *make*.

1.   I was late for the concert because there was a traffic jam.
     The traffic jam ....

2.   Why don't we go to that new bookshop in town this afternoon?
     ....

3.   How about going to see the new James Bond film?
     ....

4.   We were told we had to run 5 km by our basketball coach.
     Our basketball coach ....

 **Exam task**

3 🔊 **Track 16** A girl is having her **sixteenth birthday party** next week. Her friends want to buy her a **present**, but they don't have much **money**. Talk together about the different presents they could give her and say which would be **best**. Here is a picture with some ideas to help you.

 **Exam facts**

- In this part, the examiner describes a situation to you and shows you some pictures.
- You have to discuss your views and opinions with the other student.
- You will need to make suggestions and reply to suggestions the other student makes.

© Cambridge University Press and UCLES 2015

Go to https://www.youtube.com/user/cambridgeenglishtv to watch official Cambridge English videos of *Preliminary* and *Preliminary for Schools* Speaking tests.

Food and drink

1 Complete the dialogues with words from the box. Then, in pairs, ask and answer.

about	don't	fancy	have	shall	what	would

1. **A:** What .... we have for lunch?
   B: I think we . . .

2. **A:** How .... getting a takeaway later?
   B: No, . . .

3. **A:** Which traditional dish from your country .... you recommend trying?
   B: You should . . .

4. **A:** Why .... we cook dinner for our friends on Saturday?
   B: That's . . .

5. **A:** Let's .... a barbecue tonight!
   B: I'd rather . . .

6. **A:** Do you .... going to that new pizza restaurant this evening?
   B: Why don't we . . .

2 Complete the dialogue. Then, in pairs, take turns to be the waiter and the customer.

Customer: Hello. **(1)** (*Ask for a table.*) ....

Waiter: Of course. Follow me. Here you are.

Customer: Thank you. **(2)** (*Ask to see the menu.*) ....

Waiter: Here it is. Can I get you anything to drink while you decide?

Customer: **(3)** (*Ask for two drinks, one for you and one for your friend.*)

Waiter: Are you ready to order?

Customer: Yes. **(4)** (*Ask for two dishes, one for you and one for your friend.*)

Waiter: Is everything OK with your meal?

Customer: **(5)** (*Say one dish is fine but make a complaint about the other.*)

Waiter: Would you like any desserts or coffee?

Customer: **(6)** (*Say no and ask for the bill.*) ....

Waiter: Certainly. How would you like to pay?

Customer: **(7)** (*Tell the waiter how you would like to pay.*) ....

 **Exam task**

3

🔊 **Track 17** A group of students is having a **party** to celebrate the end of the school year. Each student has to bring some **food**. Talk together about the different **types** of food the students could bring and say which would be **best** for a class party. Here is a picture with some ideas to help you.

✓ **Exam tips**

- Show interest in what the other student says and respond to what they say.
- Look at and talk to the other student when you're speaking and not the examiner.
- At the end of the conversation, you should agree on a final decision with the other student.

Go to https://www.youtube.com/user/cambridgeenglishtv to watch official Cambridge English videos of *Preliminary* and *Preliminary for Schools* Speaking tests.

Free time

1 **Respond to statements 1–7. Use the phrases in the box.**

I agree that . . .	I believe . . .	I feel that . . . I guess . . .
I have no doubt that . . .	I'm absolutely certain that . . .	I'm (not) sure that . . .
In my opinion . . .	Personally, I (don't) think that . . .	To be honest . . .

1. Doing dangerous activities like motor-racing isn't very responsible.

....

2. Dancing's one of the most sociable activities there is.

....

3. If you keep your body fit, your mind will be healthy too.

....

4. It's really important to do activities apart from work or study.

....

5. Hanging out with friends is as important as having hobbies.

....

6. It's important to spend some time each week just doing nothing.

....

7. Playing computer games or watching TV is a waste of time.

....

2 **Choose the correct alternative.**

1. I don't want to swim outdoors today because it's *too / enough* cold.

2. Wow! That was *so / such* a good film!

3. Jenny collects action figures – she's got *so / such* many now that she's got nowhere to put them.

4. I never seem to have *too / enough* free time.

5. Adam plays the guitar *so / such* well – he should be a professional musician.

6. I'm *too / enough* busy to go out tonight.

3

Track 18 Two friends are going away for a **weekend**. Their parents will pay for them to do an **exciting new activity**. Talk together about the different activities they could do and say which would be most exciting to try for the **first time**. Here is a picture with some ideas to help you.

Get it right!

Look at the sentences below and choose the correct one.

They are such pleasant people.

They are so pleasant people.

Go to https://www.youtube.com/user/cambridgeenglishtv to watch official Cambridge English videos of *Preliminary* and *Preliminary for Schools* Speaking tests.

Transport

1 Look at the picture and complete the sentences with an appropriate preposition.

1. Four people are cycling .... the road.

2. They are in .... of the traffic.

3. The cyclist .... of the others is wearing jeans.

4. The two cyclists behind him are riding .... two taxis.

5. The taxi .... the left is grey.

6. The driver of the grey taxi is looking .... ahead.

7. .... the taxis, there is a van.

8. We can't see any passengers .... the taxis.

2 Match the questions and sentences 1–6 to the functions a–f.

1. Do you agree?	**a** interrupting politely
2. What do you think?	**b** asking whether someone has the same opinion
3. Sorry, can I say something?	**c** disagreeing
4. I'm not sure about that.	**d** asking for someone's opinion
5. Sorry, I'm not sure what you mean.	**e** agreeing
6. Exactly!	**f** asking for meaning to be made clear

3 🔊 Track 19 **Listen to the examiner explaining the Part 3 task.**

Photograph 1

Photograph 2

4 🔊 Track 20 **Now listen to the examiner explaining the Part 4 task.**

- In Part 3, the examiner gives you a large colour photo.
- You have to describe what you can see in the photo.
- You have to talk for about a minute.
- In Part 4, you have to talk to the other student about the same topic as in Part 3.
- You need to talk together for about three minutes.

© Cambridge University Press and UCLES 2015

Go to https://www.youtube.com/user/cambridgeenglishtv to watch official Cambridge English videos of *Preliminary* and *Preliminary for Schools* Speaking tests.

Travel and holidays

1 Look at the pictures of items you take on holiday. What do you think they are? Tell your partner. Use the phrases in the box.

> It could / may / might be . . .   It looks as if . . .   It looks like . . .   It's possible . . . It seems . . .

a

b

c

d

PX092

PASSENGER NAME
SMITH,JONATHAN

SEAT Nº   DEPARTURE TIME
27G   19:10

EC.CLASS
006247859
BERLIN

e

f

2 Respond to the information in 1–8. Use the phrases in the box.

Are (you)?	Did (you)?	I see.	Is he / she?	Is that right?
No way!	Oh, really?	Oh, yeah?	That's (amazing)!	Wow!

1. My uncle's climbed Mount Everest.
2. I travelled around Japan by train last year.
3. My family always goes to the beach in summer.
4. I'm going on a camping trip to the jungle next month.
5. My friend goes on extreme sports holidays every winter.
6. My brother's planning to travel around the world in a year.
7. I couldn't ride a bike because I broke my leg.
8. My sister's won a prize for one of her paintings.

☑ **Exam task**

🔊 Track 21 **Listen to the examiner explaining the Part 3 task.**

Photograph 1

Photograph 2

🔊 Track 22 **Now listen to the examiner explaining the Part 4 task.**

☑ **Exam tips**

- In Part 3, describe who you can see, where they are and what they are doing. You can also describe the clothes they are wearing and any objects you can see.
- Make sure you know how to describe position – for example, *on the left*, *on the right*, *above*, *below*, etc.
- If you don't know the word for something in the picture, don't worry. Concentrate on the things you do know.
- At the beginning of the Part 4 task, the examiner will tell you what to talk about, but they won't ask questions. You have to ask and answer questions with the other student.
- Ask the other student questions and show interest in what they say.
- Don't worry too much about making mistakes – just try to keep talking with the other student.

Go to https://www.youtube.com/user/cambridgeenglishtv to watch official Cambridge English videos of *Preliminary* and *Preliminary for Schools* Speaking tests.

House and home

1

Match the words in the box to items a–i in the house. What do you use them for?

basin

cooker

balcony

garage

gate

lamp

mirror

bookcase

stairs

2

Match 1–8 to a–h to complete the expressions.

1. I don't know what
2. I can't remember the word
3. What do you
4. I can't find the word I'm
5. I'm not sure this
6. What I
7. What's the
8. You know

a for the thing that . . .

b what I mean, it . . .

c call it . . . ?

d it's called!

e is the right word, but . . .

f looking for.

g mean is . . .

h name of the thing that . . .

3 🔊 Track 23 **Listen to the examiner explaining the Part 3 task.**

Photograph 1

Photograph 2

4 🔊 Track 24 **Now listen to the examiner explaining the Part 4 task.**

◉ **Get it right!**

Look at the sentences below. Then try to correct the mistake in each one.

I didn't know that this city can be so interesting.

It could be nice to see *The Merchant of Venice* with Al Pacino.

Go to https://www.youtube.com/user/cambridgeenglishtv to watch official Cambridge English videos of *Preliminary* and *Preliminary for Schools* Speaking tests.

 **Think about it** Preliminary Reading Part 1

Read the sentences about Preliminary Reading Part 1. Are the sentences TRUE or FALSE?

1. In this part of the exam you have to read short notices, signs and messages and choose the correct meaning. ....

2. The texts you read will all be the same kind of text. ....

3. There is an example text, and then five more texts. ....

4. There are three possible answers to choose from for each text. ....

5. Sometimes there is a question before the three options, and sometimes there are just the three options. ....

6. There is visual information such as a picture with every text. ....

7. To understand the meaning, it is important to think about the situation in which each text would appear, e.g. as a notice on a wall, or as an email. ....

8. It is also important to think about the purpose of the text, e.g. who it is for and why someone has written it. ....

 **Think about it** Preliminary Reading Part 2

Read the information about Preliminary Reading Part 2. Complete the information with the words in the box.

| all | eight | five | match | people | points | suitable | text |

In Part 2, you have to **(1)** .... people to different products, places or activities. There are **(2)** .... short descriptions of people, saying what they each want, need or are interested in. There are **(3)** .... descriptions of products, places or activities, so there are three that you don't need to match. It's a good idea to read the descriptions of the **(4)** .... first and note what each one is looking for. Each person will mention three key **(5)** .... that they are looking for. Then you can read the descriptions of the products, places or activities and find the one that is the most **(6)** .... for each person. Some points are mentioned in more than one **(7)** .... , but it's important to find the text that mentions **(8)** .... the key points a person is looking for.

 **Think about it** Preliminary Reading Part 3

Read the sentences about Preliminary Reading Part 3. Choose the correct words to complete the sentences.

1. In Part 3, you have to read a *longer / shorter* text.

2. There *might be some / won't be any* unfamiliar vocabulary in the text.

3. The questions are in the form of *five / ten* statements about the text.

4. You need to look for *general / detailed* information in the text, to decide if the statements are true or false.

5. You *have to / don't have to* understand every single word of the text.

6. On the answer sheet, you choose *A / B* if a statement is correct, and you choose *A / B* if it is incorrect.

7. The information in the text *follows / doesn't follow* the same order as the questions.

8. It's a good idea to read the ten statements *before / after* you read the text.

 **Think about it** Preliminary Reading Part 4

Read the sentences about Preliminary Reading Part 4. Choose the correct words in the brackets to complete the sentences.

1. There are .... multiple-choice questions. (five / ten)

2. There are .... options for each question. (three / four)

3. To answer the questions, you need to understand the writer's .... and attitude, as well as the information in the text. (opinion / background)

4. The first question always asks about the writer's .... in writing the text. (history / purpose)

5. The final question always asks about the .... meaning of the text. (global / detailed)

6. The three middle questions might ask about .... information in the text, or about the writer's feelings. (general / detailed)

7. The three middle questions follow the .... of the information in the text. (order / meaning)

8. It can be a good idea to leave the .... and last questions to the end, when you have answered the other questions. (first / second)

Think about it Preliminary Reading Part 5

Read the sentences about Preliminary Reading Part 5. Which TWO sentences are false?

1. Part 5 is a short text with ten gaps.

2. For each gap, there are four possible words to choose from.

3. For some gaps, there is more than one correct answer.

4. This part of the exam tests your vocabulary and some grammar, such as pronouns and modal verbs.

5. It's a good idea to read the whole text first, before you choose the correct answers.

6. The options often have similar meanings, so you need to think about how the words are used in a sentence, as well as their meanings.

7. The text may contain some high level vocabulary.

8. It's a good idea to read the text through when you have finished, to see if it makes sense with the options you have chosen.

Think about it Preliminary Writing Part 1

Read the sentences about Preliminary Writing Part 1. Are the sentences TRUE or FALSE? Correct the false sentences.

1. There are five sentences in this task. ....
....

2. The sentences are all on different topics. ....
....

3. Underneath each sentence, there is a second, gapped sentence. ....
....

4. You have to complete the second sentence so it has the same meaning as the first. ....
....

5. You must use three words. ....
....

6. You need to use some words that are not in the first sentence. ....
....

7. All the words you write must be spelled correctly, in order to get full marks. ....
....

8. It is a good idea to read the second sentence when you have completed it to make sure it has exactly the same meaning as the first. ....
....

Think about it Preliminary Writing Part 2

Read the information about Preliminary Writing Part 2. Choose the correct words to complete the information.

In Part 2, you have to write a **(1)** *short / long* message. It can be an email, a note or a text message. The

question **(2)** *tells / doesn't tell* you who you are writing to and why you are writing. The question includes

(3) *three / four* bullet points. You **(4)** *must / don't have to* answer all these points in your message. You

(5) *must / don't have to* include extra information. Your answer must be between **(6)** *30 / 35* and

(7) *45 / 55* words. If it is too long or too short, you may get a **(8)** *higher / lower* mark for the task.

Think about it Preliminary Writing Part 3

Read the information about Preliminary Writing Part 3. Complete the information with the words in the box.

100	choose	imagination	middle	mistakes	organise
reply	start	story	title	topic	vocabulary

In Part 3, you can **(1)** .... between two different tasks. You can either write an informal letter / email,

or a **(2)** .... For both tasks, you should write about **(3)** .... words. For the letter / email,

you are given part of a letter / email that someone has written to you, and you have to write a **(4)** ....

to it. It is important to deal with all the points in the letter / email to you and also add more information of your own.

For the story, you are given either the **(5)** .... of the story, or the first line. Your story must be on the

(6) .... you are given, but you can use your **(7)** .... for ideas. With both text types, it

is important to plan your answer and **(8)** .... your ideas into paragraphs. With the letter / email,

you must **(9)** .... and end it in a suitable way, with a suitable informal phrase. If you choose the

story, your story must have a clear beginning, **(10)** .... and ending. In this task, you should use a

wide range of **(11)** .... and verb forms. You will get a better mark if you try to use more difficult

language, even if you make a few **(12)** ....

 **Think about it** Preliminary Listening Part 1

Read the information about Preliminary Listening Part 1. Complete the information with the words in the box.

| vocabulary | pictures | multiple-choice | people | mark | recordings | facts |

In Preliminary Listening Part 1, you hear seven short **(1)** .... For each recording, there is one

(2) .... question to answer, and there are three **(3)** .... , A, B and C. You choose the

correct picture to answer the question. The information you hear is based on **(4)** .... Sometimes

you hear two **(5)** .... speaking, and sometimes you only hear one. All the words you hear are from the

Preliminary **(6)** .... list. You receive one **(7)** .... for each correct answer.

 **Think about it** Preliminary Listening Part 2

Read the sentences about Preliminary Listening Part 2. Are the sentences TRUE or FALSE?

1. In Part 2, you may hear two speakers or you may just hear one. ....

2. The recording in Part 2 is the same length as each recording in Part 1. ....

3. There are seven multiple-choice questions to answer. ....

4. For each question, there are three possible answers, A, B or C, for you to choose from. ....

5. The questions follow the order of information in the recording. So, you hear all of the information for question 1 before you hear the information for question 2, and so on. ....

6. There are two marks for each correct answer. ....

7. For each question, you put a cross (x) in the correct box to show your answer. ....

Think about it Preliminary Listening Part 3

Read the sentences about Preliminary Listening Part 3. Are the sentences TRUE or FALSE?

1. There are five gaps for you to complete in Part 3. ....

2. You hear one person speaking in this part. ....

3. You have to write a word or short phrase in each gap. ....

4. You should try to spell the missing words correctly. ....

5. You should try to write exactly the words you hear in the gaps. ....

6. You get one mark for every word you write in a gap. ....

   So, if you write two words, you get two marks. ....

7. Every sentence or note you read has a gap in it. ....

Think about it Preliminary Listening Part 4

Match 1–8 to a–h to make sentences about Preliminary Listening Part 4.

1. You read six

2. You have to decide whether each sentence

3. You hear

4. Sometimes you have to decide

5. To give your answers, you have to

6. If you tick box A, you think that

7. You have to listen for the speakers'

8. You get

a is true or false.

b whether the two speakers agree.

c tick one of the boxes.

d the answer to the question is YES.

e sentences in this part of the test.

f a conversation between two people.

g one mark for each correct answer.

h opinions and attitudes.

 **Think about it** Preliminary Speaking Part 1

Read the sentences about Preliminary Speaking Part 1. Are the sentences TRUE or FALSE?

1. You should talk to your partner during this part of the test. ....

2. You should give one-word answers. ....

3. The examiner may ask you questions about where you're from and what you do. ....

4. There are two phases to this part of the test. ....

5. You should ask your partner some questions about him / herself. ....

6. It's a good idea to practise spelling your name out loud before this part of the test. ....

7. If you don't understand a question, you can ask the examiner to repeat it. ....

8. The examiner will ask you some general questions, such as what you like doing in your free time, or what you enjoy about studying English. ....

 **Think about it** Preliminary Speaking Part 2

Read the information about Preliminary Speaking Part 2. Complete the information with the words in the box.

partner	opportunity	situation	interested	opinions	stop	instructions	pictures

In Part 2, the examiner will describe a **(1)** .... to you and your **(2)** .... You should listen

carefully to make sure you understand what the examiner says. The examiner will ask you to look at some

(3) .... The examiner will then repeat the **(4)** .... about what you have to do. Then, you have

to talk to your partner. Don't forget to ask for his or her **(5)** .... Remember to listen to what your partner

says, and show that you are **(6)** .... in what they have to say. Make sure you give your partner enough

(7) .... to speak, and interrupt politely if he / she talks too much. You should keep talking until the

examiner asks you to **(8)** ....

Think about it   Preliminary Speaking Part 3

Match 1–8 to a–h to make sentences about Preliminary Speaking Part 3.

1. In Part 3, you have to describe

2. You will see a

3. You should describe everything

4. You should not talk

5. If there's something you don't know the word for,

6. Don't stop talking

7. Don't worry about making

8. Try not to compare yourself with your partner –

a you can see in the picture.

b describe it using other words.

c until the examiner asks you to.

d about things or ideas which are not in the picture.

e a picture.

f the examiner assesses each of you individually.

g different picture from your partner.

h mistakes – just keep talking!

Think about it   Preliminary Speaking Part 4

Complete each sentence about Preliminary Speaking Part 4 by choosing the correct option.

1. In Part 4 you talk about

a the same topic as Part 3.

b the same topic as Part 2.

2. During Part 4, you should talk to

a the examiner.

b your partner.

3. You should

a ask your partner questions.

b wait for the examiner to ask you questions.

4. If you aren't sure what to say next, you could

a ask your partner for their opinion.

b ask the examiner what to do.

5. It's important to show that

a you know more than your partner about the topic.

b you are listening to what your partner is saying.

6. You should make sure that you

a talk as much as possible.

b give your partner a chance to speak.

7. Remember to

a talk about everything the examiner asks you to talk about.

b choose one of the options the examiner asks you to talk about.

8. You should try not to

a ask the examiner to repeat the instructions.

b sit in silence. If you need to, ask the examiner to repeat the instructions.

Clothes and Accessories

backpack	go (with/together)	perfume	sweatshirt
bag	**(phr v)**	plastic	swimming costume
belt	handbag	pocket	take off
blouse	handkerchief	pullover	tie
boot	hat	purse	tights
bracelet	jacket	put on	tracksuit
button	jeans	raincoat	trainers
cap	jewellery / jewelry	ring	trousers
chain	jumper	scarf	T-shirt
clothes	kit	shirt	sandal
coat	knit	shoe	sweatshirt
collar	label	shorts	swimsuit
cotton	laundry	silk	try on
dress	leather	size	umbrella
earring	make-up	skirt	underpants
fashion	match **(v)**	sleeve(less)	underwear
fasten	material	socks	undress
fit **(v)**	necklace	stripe	uniform
fold **(v)**	old-fashioned **(adj)**	suit	wallet
glasses	pants	sunglasses	watch
glove	pattern	sweater	wear (out)
			wool(len)

Colours

(dark/light/pale)	gold	orange	silver
black	golden	pink	yellow
blue	green	purple	white
brown	grey	red	

Communications and Technology

access	disc/disk	keyboard	ring
address	dot	laptop (computer)	ring up
at!@	download **(n & v)**	machine	screen
blog	drag	message	server
blogger	DVD (player)	mobile phone	software
by post	electronic(s)	mouse	switch off
calculator	email	mouse mat	switch on
call **(v)**	engaged	MP3 player	talk
call back	enter	net	telephone
CD (player)	envelope	online	text
CD-Rom	equipment	operator	text message
chat	fax	parcel	turn off
chat room	file	password	turn on
click **(v)**	hang up	PC	upload
computer	hardware	phone	video clip
connect	headline	photograph	volume
connection	homepage	photography	web
delete	install	postcard	web page
dial	internet	print	webcam
dial up	invent	printer	website
digital	invention	program(me)	
digital camera	IT	reply	

Education

absent	bookshelf	composition	essay
advanced	break up	course	geography
arithmetic	break(time)	curriculum	handwriting
art	certificate	degree	history
beginner	chemistry	desk	homework
bell	class	dictionary	information
biology	classroom	diploma	instructions
blackboard	clever	drama	instructor
board	coach	economics	intermediate
book	college	elementary	IT

know	nature studies	qualification	study **(v)**
laboratory (lab)	note	read	subject
language	notice board	register	teach
learn	pencil case	remember	teacher
lesson	photography	rubber	technology
level	physics	ruler	term
library	practice **(n)**	school	test
mark	practise **(v)**	science	university
math(s)	primary school	secondary school	
mathematics	project	student	
music	pupil	studies	

Entertainment and Media

act **(v)**	classical music	group	orchestra
action	comedy	guitar	paint
actor	comic	guitarist	painter
actress	competition	headline	perform
ad	concert	hero	performance
admission	dance	heroine	performer
adventure	dancer	hip hop	play
advert	disc	hit song	poem
advertisement	disco	horror	pop music
art	display	instrument	programme
article	DJ / disc jockey	interval	quiz
audience	documentary	interview(er)	recording
ballet	drama	jazz music	review
band	draw	journalist	rock music
board game	drawing	keyboard	romantic
book	DVD (player)	laugh	row
camera	entrance	listen to	scene
card	exhibition	look at	screen
cartoon	exit	magazine	series
CD (player)	festival	magic	soap opera
CD-Rom	film	MP3 player	stage
celebrity	film maker	museum	star
channel	film star	music	studio
chat show	fireworks	musician	talk show
chess	folk music	news	television
cinema	fun	newspaper	thriller
circus	go out	opera	video

Environment

bottle bank	litter	public transport	recycling
climate change	petrol **(Br Eng)**	recycle	rubbish (bin)
gas **(Am Eng)**	pollution	recycled	traffic jam

Food and Drink

apple	cabbage	cooker	flour
bake **(v)**	cafe	cookie	food
banana	cafeteria	corn	fork
barbecue **(n & v)**	cake	cream	French fries
bean	can (of beans)	cucumber	fresh
biscuit	candy	cup	fridge
bitter **(adj)**	canteen	curry	fried
boil **(v)**	carrot	cut	fruit
boiled	cereal	delicious	fruit juice
bottle	cheese	dessert	fry
bowl	chef	diet	frying pan
box	chicken	dinner	garlic
bread	chilli	dish	glass
break	chips	drink	grape
breakfast	chocolate	duck	grill **(n & v)**
broccoli	coconut	eat	grilled
bunch (of bananas)	coffee	egg	herbs
burger	cola	fish	honey
butter	cook **(n & v)**	flavour	hot

hungry
ice
ice cream
ingredients
jam
jug
juice
kitchen
knife
lamb
lemon
lemonade
lettuce
lunch
main course
meal
meat
melon
menu
microwave (n)
milk

mineral water
mushroom
oil
omelette
onion
orange
pan
pasta
pea
peach
peanut
pear
pepper
picnic
pie
piece of cake
pineapple
pizza
plate
potato
recipe

refreshments
rice
roast (v & adj)
roll
salad
salmon
salt
sandwich
sauce
saucepan
saucer
sausage
slice (n)
snack
soft drink
soup
sour
spicy
spinach
spoon
steak

strawberry
sugar
sweet (adj & n)
takeaway
taste
tasty
tea
thirsty
toast
tomato
tuna
turkey
vegetable
vegetarian
waiter
waitress
wash up
yog(h)urt

Health, Medicine and Exercise

accident
ache
ambulance
ankle
appointment
arm
aspirin
baby
bandage
bleed (v)
blood (n)
body
bone
brain
break
breath
breathe
check
chemist
chin
clean
cold (n)
comb
cough (n & v)
cut
damage

danger
dangerous
dead
dentist
die
diet
doctor
ear
earache
emergency
exercise
eye
face
fall
feel better/ill/sick
fever
finger
fit
flu
foot
get better/worse
go jogging
gym
gymnastics
hair
hand

head
headache
health
hear
heart
heel
hospital
hurt
ill
illness
injure
keep fit
knee
leg
lie down
medicine
nose
nurse
operate
operation
pain
painful
patient (n)
pharmacy
pill
prescription

problem
recover
rest (n & v)
run
shoulder
sick
skin
soap
sore throat
stomach
stomach ache
stress
swim
tablet
take exercise
temperature
thumb
tired
toes
tooth
toothache
toothbrush
walk
well (adj)

Hobbies and Leisure

barbecue
beach
bicycle
bike
camera
camp
camping
campsite
CD (player)
chess
club
collect(or)
collection
computer
cruise

dance
dancing
doll
draw
drawing
DVD (player)
facilities
fan
festival
fiction
gallery
go out
guitar
hang out
hire

hobby
holidays
jogging
join in
keen on
keep fit
magazine
member(ship)
model
museum
music
musician
nightlife
opening hours
paint

painting
park
party
photograph
picnic
playground
quiz
sculpture
sightseeing
slide
sunbathe
tent

House and Home

accommodation
address
air conditioning
alarm (fire/car)
alarm clock
antique
apartment
armchair
balcony
basin
bath(tub)
bathroom
bed
bedroom
bell
bin
blanket
blind
block
(notice) board
bookcase
bookshelf
bowl
box
brush
bucket
bulb
candle
carpet
ceiling
cellar
central heating
chair
channel (with TV)
chest of drawers
clock

computer
cooker
cottage
cupboard
curtain
cushion
desk
digital (adj)
dining room
dish
dishwasher
door
downstairs
drawer
dustbin
duvet
DVD (player)
electric(al)
entrance
fan
flat
flatmate
floor
freezer
fridge
frying pan
furniture
garage
garden
gas
gate
grill
ground (floor)
hall
handle
heat (v)

heater
heating
hi-fi
home
house
housewife
housework
iron
jug
kettle
key
kitchen
ladder
lamp
laptop (computer)
lift
light
(clothes) line
living-room
lock
microwave (n)
mirror
mug
neighbour
oil
oven
pan
path
pillow
pipe
plant
plug
plug in
property
radio
refrigerator

remote control
rent
repair
roof
room
roommate
rubbish
safe (adj)
seat
sheet
shelf
shower
sink
sitting room
sofa
stairs
stay (v)
step
surround
switch
table
tap
telephone
television
toilet
towel
tower
toy
TV (screen/set)
upstairs (adv)
vase
video
wall
washing machine
window

Language

advanced
answer
argue
ask
beginner
chat
communicate
communication

elementary
email
grammar
intermediate
joke
letter
mean
meaning

mention
message
pronounce
pronunciation
question
say
sentence
shout

speak
talk
tell
translate
translation
vocabulary
word

Personal Feelings, Opinions and Experiences (Adjectives)

able
afraid
alone
amazed
amazing
amusing
angry
annoyed
anxious
ashamed
awful
bad
beautiful
better
bored
boring
bossy

brave
brilliant
busy
calm
careful
challenging
charming
cheerful
clear
clever
confident
confused
confusing
cool
crazy
cruel
curious

cute
delighted
depressed
different
difficult
disappointed
disappointing
easy
embarrassed
embarrassing
excellent
excited
exciting
famous
fantastic
favourite
fine

fit
fond
free
friendly
frightened
funny
generous
gentle
glad
good
great
guilty
happy
hard
healthy
heavy

hungry	noisy	relaxed	sure
important	normal	reliable	surprised
intelligent	old	rich	sweet
interested	old-fashioned	right	tall
interesting	ordinary	rude	terrible
jealous	original	sad	tired
keen	patient	satisfied	true
kind	personal	serious	typical
lazy	pleasant	slim	unable
lovely	poor	slow	unhappy
lucky	positive	small	unusual
mad	pretty	smart	useful
married	quick	soft	well
miserable	quiet	sorry	wonderful
modern	ready	special	worried
negative	real	strange	wrong
nervous	realistic	strong	young
nice	reasonable	stupid	

Places: Buildings

apartment block / apartment building	cottage	hotel	shop
	department store	house	sports centre
bank	disco	library	stadium
bookshop	elevator	lift	supermarket
bookstore	entrance	museum	swimming pool
building	exit	office	theatre
cafe	factory	palace	tourist information centre
cafeteria	flat	police station	
castle	gallery	pool	
cinema	garage	post office	tower
clinic	grocery store	prison	university
club	guest-house	railway station	
college	hospital	ruin	
		school	

Places: Countryside

area	field	path	sea
bay	forest	port	seaside
beach	harbour	railway	sky
campsite	hill	rainforest	stream
canal	island	region	valley
cliff	lake	river	village
desert	land	rock	waterfall
earth	mountain	sand	wood
farm	ocean	scenery	

Places: Town and City

apartment building	cashpoint	park	square
	city centre	pavement	station
airport	corner	petrol station	street
booking office	crossing	playground	subway
bridge	crossroads	road	town
bus station	fountain	roundabout	tunnel
bus stop	market	route	turning
car park	motorway	shopping centre	underground
cash machine	monument	signpost	zoo

Services

bank	doctor	library	swimming pool
cafe	gallery	museum	theatre
cafeteria	garage	post office	tourist information
cinema	hairdresser	restaurant	
dentist	hotel	sports centre	

Shopping

ad
advert
advertise
advertisement
assistant
bargain
bill
book
buy
cash
cent
change
cheap
cheque
choose

close (v)
closed
collect
complain
cost (n & v)
credit card
customer
damaged
dear
department
    store
deposit
dollar
euro
exchange

expensive
for sale
hire
inexpensive
label
logo
luxury
money
order
pay (for)
penny
pound
price
reasonable
receipt

reduce
reduced
rent
reserve
return
save
second-hand
sell
shop
shop assistant
shopper
shopping
spend
supermarket
try on

Sport

athlete
athletics
badminton
ball
baseball
basketball
bat
bathing suit
beach
bicycle
bike
boat
boxing
catch (v)
champion
championship
changing room
climb (v)
climbing
club
coach (n)
compete
competition
competitor
contest
court
cricket
cycling
cyclist
dancing
diving
enter (a competition)

extreme sports
(sports) facilities
fishing
fitness
football
football player
game
goal
goalkeeper
golf
gym
gymnastics
helmet
high jump
hit (v)
hockey
horse-riding
ice hockey
ice skating
instructor
jogging
join in
kick (v)
kit
league
locker (room)
long jump
luck
match
member
motor-racing
net
play (v)

point(s)
practice (n)
practise (v)
prize
race
race track
racing
racket
reserve (n)
rest (n & v)
ride (n & v)
rider
riding
rugby
run (n & v)
running
sail (n & v)
sailing
score
sea
season
shoot(ing)
shorts
skateboard
skating
skiing
snowboard
snowboarding
soccer
sport(s)
sports centre
squash
stadium

surf
surfboard
surfboarding
surfing
swim
swimming
swimming
    costume
swimmng pool
swimsuit
table tennis
take part
team
tennis
tennis player
throw (v)
ticket
tired
track
tracksuit
trainer(s)
train(ing)
versus / v
volleyball
walk (v)
watch (v)
water skiing
win
workout
yoga

The Natural World

air
animal
autumn
beach
bee
bird
branch
bush
butterfly
cave
cliff
climate

coast
continent
country
countryside
desert
dolphin
donkey
duck
earth
east
elephant
environment

environmental
explore(r)
fall (Am Eng)
farmland
field
fire
fish
flood
flower
forest
freeze
frog

fur
giraffe
grass
grow
hill
hot
ice
island
jungle
kangaroo
lake
land

leaf	plant	south	valley
lion	pollution	space	water
monkey	rabbit	spring	waterfall
moon	rainforest	star	waves
mosquito	range	stone	west
mountain	river	summer	wild
mouse/mice	rock	sun	wildlife
nature	sand	sunrise	winter
north	scenery	sunset	wood
parrot	sea	sunshine	wool
penguin	shark	tiger	world
planet	sky	tree	zebra

Time

afternoon	evening	monthly	today
am / pm	half (past)	morning	tomorrow
appointment	holidays	night	tonight
autumn	hour	noon	week
birthday	January - December	o'clock	weekday
century	meeting	past	weekend
clock	midnight	quarter (past / to)	weekly
daily	minute	second	winter
date	moment	spring	working hours
day	Monday - Sunday	summer	year
diary	month	time	yesterday

Travel and Transport

abroad	change (v)	fuel	overnight
accommodation	charter	garage	park (v)
(aero) / (air)plane	check in (v)	gas / gas station	parking lot
airline	check-in (n)	(Am Eng)	parking space
airport	check out (v)	gate	passenger
ambulance	coach	guest	passport
announcement	confirm	guide	path
arrival	country	guidebook	petrol
arrive	crossing	handlebars	petrol station
at sea	crossroads	harbour	pilot
backpack	currency	helicopter	platform
backpacker	customs	hitchhike	public transport
backpacking	cycle (n & v)	hotel	railroad
bag	cyclist	immigration	railway
baggage	delay	jet	reception
bicycle / bike	delayed	journey	repair (v)
board (v)	deliver	land (v)	reservation
boarding pass	depart	leave	reserve
boat	departure	left	return (n & v)
border	destination	light	ride
bridge	direction	lorry	road sign
brochure	document(s)	luggage	roundabout
bus	dollar	machine	route
bus station	double room	map	sail (v)
bus stop	drive	mechanic	scooter
by air	driver	mirror	(bus) service
by land	driving/driver's licence	miss	ship
by rail	due	motorbike	sightseeing
by road	duty-free	motorway	signpost
by sea	embassy	move	single room
cab	euro	nationality	speed
cabin	exchange rate	oil	subway
canal	facilities	on board	suitcase
capital city	far	on business	take off
car	fare	on foot	taxi
car alarm	ferry	on holiday	tour (n & v)
car park	flight	on time	tour guide
case	fly	on vacation	tourist
catch (v)	foreign	operator	tourist information centre

traffic
traffic jam
traffic lights
train
tram
translate

translation
travel
trip
tunnel
tyre/tire
underground

underground train
vehicle
visa
visit(or)
waiting room
way

wheel
window
windscreen

Weather

blow
breeze
cloud
cloudy
cold
cool
degrees
dry
fog
foggy

forecast
freezing
frozen
gale
get wet
heat
hot
humid
ice
icy

lightning
mild
rain
shower
snow
snowfall
storm
sun
sunny
sunshine

temperature
thunder(storm)
warm
weather
wet
wind
windy

Work and Jobs

actor
actress
application
apply
architect
army
artist
assistant
athlete
babysitter
banker
boss
break (n)
businessman
businesswoman
butcher
cameraman
candidate
canteen
captain
career
chef
chemist
cleaner
colleague
company
computer
conference
contract
cook
crew
customs officer
CV
dancer
dentist

department
designer
desk
detective
diary
diploma
director
diver
doctor
earn
email
employ (v)
employee
employer
employment
engineer
explorer
factory
farm
farmer
film star
fireman
football player/footballer
full time
goalkeeper
guard
guest
guide
hairdresser
housewife
housework
instructions
instructor
job
journalist

judge
king
laboratory
lawyer
lecturer
letter
librarian
manager
mechanic
meeting
message
model
musician
novelist
nurse
occupation
office
officer (e.g. prison/police)
out of work
owner
painter
part time
photographer
pilot
poet
policeman
police officer
policewoman
politician
porter
postman
president
profession
professional
professor

(computer) programmer
publisher
qualification
queen
quit
receptionist
reporter
retire
retirement
sailor
salary
sales assistant
salesman
saleswoman
scientist
secretary
security guard
shop assistant
shopper
singer
soldier
staff
student
taxi driver
teacher
tennis player
tour guide
trade
travel agent
unemployed
uniform
wage(s)
waiter/waitress
work
worker

ANSWER KEY

Reading Part 1:1

1a 1 Is the sun shining at the moment?
2 Why are you studying English this year?
3 How often do they meet their friends?
4 Are you looking forward to next weekend?
5 Does she like watching films?
6 Where does your brother live?

1b 1 d 2 c 3 e 4 b 5 a 6 f

2 1 wake up, awake   4 leave, late
2 have, morning   5 go, buy
3 clean, routine   6 go, weekend

3 1 C 2 B 3 A 4 B 5 A

Reading Part 1:2

1 1 up   2 in   3 over   4 out
5 out   6 back   7 together 8 out

2 1 a 2 b 3 a 4 a
5 b 6 b 7 a 8 b

3 1 C 2 C 3 B 4 C 5 A

Reading Part 1:3

1 1 club   6 galleries
2 hobby   7 sunbathing
3 dancing   8 magazine
4 festival   9 photography
5 sightseeing 10 member

2 1 Do you agree that
2 not sure, because
3 What I mean is
4 that's an interesting point
5 like I said
6 What do you think about this
7 going back to
8 On a completely different subject

3 1 C 2 A 3 B 4 A 5 B

Get it right!
I**'m writing** to you because last week I started a new English course in the same school.

Reading Part 2:1

1 1 heart, beats   4 break, ambulance
2 doctors, fit   5 sick, medicine
3 dangerous, rugby   6 injury, rest

2 1 have to   3 needn't   5 ought to
2 shouldn't   4 mustn't   6 should

3 1 C 2 D 3 E 4 H 5 G

Reading Part 2:2

1 1 drama   3 order   5 sculptures
2 stage   4 horror   6 videos

2 1 Where did you go on holiday last year?
2 No, she's just left.
3 I've already done it.
4 When did you move to this town?

3 1 F 2 G 3 A 4 H 5 C

Reading Part 2:3

1 1 resort   3 accommodation
2 facilities   4 reservation

2 1 arrived
2 're / are having
3 've / have already done
4 went
5 haven't seen

3 1 G 2 B 3 A 4 D 5 C

Get it right!
Yesterday I bought some clothes

Reading Part 3:1

1 1 Maths is my favourite subject.
2 Sam is often late for appointments.
3 Photography is a very popular hobby.
4 Mrs Edwards usually teaches us.
5 This work isn't good enough!
6 Miss Jones isn't as strict as Mr Brown.
7 The test was too difficult for me.
8 I had my work checked by a friend.
9 We have just finished eating.
10 I haven't seen that film yet.

2 1 B 2 A 3 A 4 B 5 B
6 A 7 B 8 B 9 B 10 A

3 1 attending   4 range   7 set
2 dreams   5 follow   8 provide
3 go on   6 feel

Reading Part 3:2

1 1 c 2 e 3 a 4 f
5 h 6 g 7 b 8 d

2 1 for   2 around   3 on   4 up
5 with   6 out   7 back   8 for

3 1 B 2 A 3 B 4 A 5 A
6 B 7 B 8 A 9 B 10 B

Reading Part 3:3

1 1 parrot   6 bee
2 lion   7 giraffe
3 shark   8 cow
4 dolphin   9 cat
5 dinosaur   10 camel

2 1 small, white, farm
 2 small, round, black
 3 tiny, colourful, African
 4 large, shy, wild
 5 lovely, soft, brown
 6 small, shiny, blue

3 1 B   2 A   3 B   4 A   5 B
 6 B   7 B   8 A   9 B   10 B

Get it right!

I have just bought a **big new** lamp for my bedroom.

Reading Part 4:1

1 1 office   4 hospital
 2 guest-house   5 factory
 3 prison   6 cottage

2 1 the way to   4 is it far
 2 Turn   5 straight on
 3 in front   6 on

3 1 C   2 C   3 B   4 C   5 B

Reading Part 4:2

1 1 climate
 2 public transport, pollution
 3 rubbish, recycle
 4 bottle bank

2 1 C   2 D   3 D   4 B   5 A

3 1 's / is going to rain   4 won't mind
 2 will be   5 'm / am going to fail
 3 's / is going to fall   6 'll / will come

Reading Part 4:3

1 1 to   2 of   3 for   4 at
 5 in   6 of   7 on   8 for

2 1 D   2 C   3 C   4 A   5 B

3 1 team   4 take part   7 competitors
 2 coach   5 win   8 trained
 3 competition   6 stadium

Get it right!

I'm sure that you will have a great holiday here.

Reading Part 5:1

1 1 classical   6 plays
 2 performed   7 exhibition
 3 Orchestra   8 Museum
 4 comedy   9 Admission
 5 audience

2 1 A   2 C   3 B   4 B   5 D
 6 A   7 B   8 D   9 A   10 C

3 Students' own answers.

Reading Part 5:2

1 1 c   2 g   3 e   4 a
 5 h   6 d   7 b   8 f

2 1 leaves   5 will probably go
 2 'm going to book   6 're going to have
 3 'm travelling   7 starts
 4 'll carry   8 'm leaving

3 1 C   2 A   3 B   4 D   5 A
 6 B   7 C   8 A   9 C   10 D

Reading Part 5:3

1 1 freezing   4 thunder   7 humid
 2 ice   5 heat   8 showers
 3 lightning   6 dry

2 1 A   2 C   3 B   4 D   5 B
 6 A   7 A   8 B   9 D   10 D

3 1 didn't have; second   5 would be; second
 2 hits; zero   6 won't be; first
 3 stays; first   7 will go / 'll go; first
 4 hear; zero   8 had; second

Get it right!

If I were you, I **would** go to the countryside because it is a lovely place and it is very peaceful.

Writing Part 1:1

1 1 the big department store was
 2 she was slowly starting to find her
 3 he had been there; he hadn't bought
 4 people her age would love
 5 Anna / her that you could buy
 6 Anna / her that it was; she (that) had spent too much
 7 he never went / goes
 8 that Anna / she should go; for herself

2 1 was sent / received / got
 2 was a sale
 3 long enough
 4 as colourful as
 5 You should / You could / I suggest you

3 1 d   2 h   3 e   4 g   5 a
 6 j   7 i   8 b   9 f   10 c

Writing Part 1:2

1 1 was in
 2 he was planning to
 3 she could take a photo
 4 know when his next film was / is
 5 he had any plans for
 6 he had enjoyed filming in
 7 he was pleased with his
 8 he would move back to

2 1 for five
   2 keen to
   3 stand spending
   4 the same
   5 less sociable

3 1 short, bossy
   2 reliable, generous
   3 cheerful, positive
   4 smart, relaxed
   5 lazy, slim
   6 confident, brave

Writing Part 1:3

1 1 terrible
   2 blew
   3 fall
   4 miserable
   5 terrified
   6 shining
   7 delighted
   8 flood

2 1 the hottest
   2 not to
   3 stay / be
   4 enough rain
   5 are encouraged

3 1 C   2 A   3 B   4 A   5 A   6 B
   7 C   8 C

Get it right!
My mom also told me to buy some T-shirts.

Writing Part 2:1

1a 1 magazine
   2 celebrity
   3 fiction
   4 controller
   5 report
   6 level
   7 board
   8 graphics
   9 article
   10 series

1b Students' own answers

2 1 I'm emailing you about the trip to the cinema on Saturday.
   2 I'm afraid
   3 I'm afraid I can't go because I'm going to visit my sister in London.
   4 Maybe you could come round to my house on Sunday and we could watch a film together?
   5 because, and

3 *Sample answer*
Hi George,
I'm writing about Friday. You wanted to go to the cinema together, remember? I'm sorry, but I can't come because my grandparents are coming to visit. You could come to my house on Sunday instead? We could watch the new Bond movie.
Freddie

Writing Part 2:2

1a A
   1 up
   2 onion
   3 Add
   4 fresh
   5 fry
   6 Serve
   7 roll
   8 spicy

B
   1 vegetables
   2 saucepan
   3 butter
   4 Cook
   5 cover
   6 boil
   7 smooth
   8 Stir

1b A 3   B 1

2 *Sample answer*
Hi Jenna,
I went to an amazing new café in town last weekend. They serve delicious pizzas and pasta. The best thing is the desserts – the chocolate cake is delicious! Are you free on Friday? We could go there together if you like.
Amy

3 1 a
   2 the
   3 –
   4 –
   5 any
   6 plenty of
   7 much
   8 some

Writing Part 2:3

1 1 First
   2 Then
   3 Next
   4 five minutes later
   5 suddenly
   6 By the time
   7 before
   8 After
   9 Finally

2 *Sample answer*
Hi Tom,
I've just got back from my holiday in Spain. It was amazing! The beaches were fantastic, and I loved the food. The people were friendly, too. Would you like to see my photos? I can email them to you if you want.
Ellie

3 1 check
   2 put
   3 put
   4 got
   5 got
   6 checked
   7 took
   8 set
   9 held

Get it right!
He taught me **many** things which I didn't know before.

Writing Part 3:1

1a 1 get on
   2 in common
   3 annoying
   4 disagree
   5 arguments
   6 respect
   7 relationship
   8 share
   9 similar
   10 ask

1b 1 go out with; C
   2 keep smiling; A
   3 Getting angry; positive; B

2 1 Hi, Jodie

2 You love sport, so why don't you join a sports club? That would be a great way to meet people. As soon as you know some people, you could organise a barbecue – that would be fun!

3 I've got a few old friends from when I lived in London. We stay in contact online. We send messages and photos to each other, and try to meet up when we can.

4 Three from: I'm, you're, you'll, don't, I've

5 glad, amazing, great, fun, old; absolutely

6 present simple: the weather looks, you love, you know, I've got, we stay, we send, we try; present continuous: you're enjoying; past simple: I lived; *will*: you'll soon make friends; *would*: that would be a great way, that would be fun

7 why don't you ...? you could ...

8 so (why don't you join ...), As soon as (you know ...), and (we try to meet up)

9 Take care and write soon! Love,

3 *Sample answer*

Hi George,

I'm sorry to hear about your problems with your family. I usually get on really well with my parents, although we don't agree about everything and we sometimes have arguments. I've only got one brother, and we are very different. We don't have much in common, but I'm fond of him and we don't often argue. I think you should avoid having serious discussions with your dad if you never agree. Little sisters can be difficult, but just be patient. I'm sure you'll get on better when she grows up. Take care and write soon,

Adele

Writing Part 3:2

1 1 paragraph A

2 paragraph B

3 paragraph C

4 past continuous: was making, was waiting; past perfect: had always wanted, had made

5 First, Next, finally

6 delighted, nervously, perfect, happy, unfortunately, fantastic, proud

2 1 hadn't learned

2 played

3 appeared

4 was singing

5 had always wanted

6 was working

7 asked

8 had heard

3 *Sample answer*

I saw the advert for a talent show, and decided to apply. I had always enjoyed singing, and I dreamed of becoming a star.

I prepared well. First, I chose a great song. Next, I practised until I knew my song perfectly. Finally, the big day came. However, while I was waiting to go on stage, I heard another singer – she was singing my song, really beautifully! I knew immediately that I wasn't as good as her!

My performance went well, and I was pleased that I had done my best. I didn't win the show, but I will always be pleased that I took part!

Writing Part 3:3

1 1 d   2 f   3 h   4 a   5 g

6 c   7 j   8 b   9 e   10 i

2 2 They were on holiday in Portugal.

3 Their flat always looked clean and beautiful.

5 First, I didn't take my shoes off before I went in.

6 As a result, I walked mud all over the carpet.

7 Then I decided to water their plants.

8 However, I spilled water all over the sofa.

9 Luckily, I managed to clean up all the mess.

10 They came back after a lovely holiday.

11 They never knew what problems I had had.

3 *Sample answer*

A new home

Last month, I went to visit my brother in his new flat. He had moved in a week before and had invited me for dinner.

When I arrived at the large apartment building, I rang the bell of the flat on the third floor, but no one answered. First, I thought he was out, so I decided to wait. Then, after an hour, I began to get worried. What had happened to him? Finally, I decided to check his address. I couldn't believe it – he lived on the fourth floor!

I went upstairs immediately. Luckily, my brother and his flatmates found it funny, and we enjoyed a lovely dinner together.

Get it right!

He said that he was **interested** in visiting my house.

Listening Part 1:1

1 1 done

2 playing / going to play

3 goes

4 played

5 do

6 went

7 did

8 been

2 1 C   2 A   3 A   4 C

5 B   6 C   7 B

Narrator: 🔊 **Track 1 Listening Part 1 Worksheet 1**

There are seven questions in this part. For each question there are three pictures and a short recording. For each question, choose the correct answer (A, B or C).

Narrator: **1 What did the man do at the sports centre yesterday?**

Man: I went along to that new sports centre yesterday evening.

Woman: Oh, yeah? Is it any good?

Man: Well, I haven't become a member yet, but they showed me around. It was pretty good. I was thinking of joining so that I could do diving lessons, but there's no pool. So, I don't know.

Woman: Oh, that's a shame. Did you try any of the facilities while you were there?

Man: I did a quick workout in the gym at the sports centre – the machines are great. You'd like it 'cos they have a running track outside.

Woman: Interesting! I'll go and take a look.

Narrator: Now listen again.

Narrator: **2 Which sport does the woman compete in?**

Man: Are you into sport, Julie?

Woman: Yeah, I've loved it since I was little and I've competed in a few different things.

Man: Oh, really? Do you mean in team sports?

Woman: Well, I play football, but only for fun with my friends. I preferred baseball when I was at school – I was quite good at it, and I almost played in a national tournament once. But no, I'm actually hoping to go out to Spain to take part in the surfing championships next month.

Man: That sounds amazing! I wish you the best of luck.

Woman: Thanks!

Narrator: Now listen again.

Narrator: **3 Where will the friends go running this evening?**

Man: I'm not as fit as I used to be. I need to start doing some training again.

Woman: Well, why don't you come for a run with me this evening after college? I usually set off from home around six o'clock. We could go along a path through the woods near college. Or we could go into the countryside, which is what I do. There's a

path by the river – it's more peaceful than running through the streets, and there are some beautiful views.

Man: Well, OK, then. Why not?

Narrator: Now listen again.

Narrator: **4 Which winter sport was Max good at when he was young?**

Woman: I'm going snowboarding next week – have you ever tried it, Max?

Man: Not since I entered a competition when I was a teenager. It didn't end well – I came last and injured my ankle!

Woman: Oh – that doesn't sound good.

Man: Well, no, it wasn't. I used to be one of the fastest skiers I knew when I was that age – my family lived in Switzerland for a few years, so I just expected to be good at other winter sports, too – like snowboarding and ice hockey. But I failed to get into the school team for that!

Woman: Really?

Narrator: Now listen again.

Narrator: **5 What did the girl lose?**

Man: Good morning, Highfield Sports Centre.

Girl: Oh, hi. My name's Charlotte. I was playing squash at the centre yesterday. I wonder if anyone's found one of my trainers? It's got 'Charlotte' in it – I was on court three with my friend. I usually put everything in my backpack with my racket. I've got one but the other isn't there. Fortunately, they aren't new, but if you could look for me, that would be great.

Man: OK. Just let me check for you … Yes, it's here!

Girl: Oh, fantastic – I'll come in later, then.

Narrator: Now listen again.

Narrator: **6 Which sports instructor is the man going to meet today?**

Man: Oh, hi, it's David. You know we said we'd meet at the sailing club later this afternoon? Well, the thing is, I forgot that I've already got an appointment at the golf club. My son, Tom, is thinking about joining so I wanted to show him around. We're also going to meet the coach. I want to ask a few questions. Tom plays a lot of football and I'm not sure it will be easy for him to do both sports. Can we meet another day instead? Sorry about this.

Narrator: Now listen again.

Narrator:	**7 What will open at the sports centre soon?**
Woman:	Good afternoon, everybody. This is a club news announcement. I know some of you are already enjoying the brand new outdoor athletics area, but if you haven't been there yet, do try it! I'm sure you're also looking forward to the basketball competition in a few weeks as well – don't forget to buy a ticket at reception if you'd like to watch. And if you want to be one of the first people to try out the climbing wall, come and book a session! You'll be able to do that from the 31st of this month.
Narrator:	Now listen again.

3
1	the strongest	4	the most exciting
2	the most challenging	5	more tiring
3	the hardest	6	more reasonable

Listening Part 1:2

1
1	check-in	5	security
2	luggage	6	departure
3	boarding pass	7	destination
4	documents	8	customs

2 1 C   2 C   3 B   4 A   5 B
6 A   7 A

Narrator:	🔊 **Track 2 Listening Part 1 Worksheet 2**
	There are seven questions in this part. For each question there are three pictures and a short recording. For each question, choose the correct answer (A, B or C).
Narrator:	**1 What time will the flight to Brussels leave?**
Girl:	Dad – we've just had an email from the airline.
Man:	Oh?
Girl:	Yeah – the time's changed for our flight to Brussels. It's something to do with a new timetable or something. There's only a few minutes difference – we were flying out at 11.57 pm, but now it's five past midnight. And the return flight the following Tuesday is now at two minutes past midnight. That's a full two hours later than it was – so we might need to change our booking at the airport car park.

Man:	OK.
Narrator:	Now listen again.
Narrator:	**2 What does the man enjoy most about flying?**
Woman:	Do you enjoy flying?
Man:	It's not my favourite thing to do. I get a bit nervous sometimes – usually when I'm just getting on board and finding my seat. It's thinking about taking off – I'm not frightened exactly, but I do feel a bit strange and I'm not keen on that. Landing's the most exciting bit. I think it's because there's usually a new place to explore. When I'm up in the air during the flight, I just find it a bit dull.
Narrator:	Now listen again.
Narrator:	**3 Where will Maggie's family stay on holiday this year?**
Man:	Are you taking the family to Italy again on holiday this year, Maggie?
Woman:	Yeah – we were thinking about going back to the same cottage we rented last summer, but it's already booked on the dates we wanted to go, unfortunately. The kids really want to go camping – there's a fantastic site in the same area with a pool and everything. But it's not really my thing, so we've reserved a family room at the hotel next door instead – there's a pool there too and it'll be much more comfortable, so it's the perfect solution!
Narrator:	Now listen again.
Narrator:	**4 What has the woman left behind?**
Woman:	Oh, no! I knew I'd leave something behind!
Man:	Don't tell me you haven't got our passports – there isn't enough time for us to go home and come back again.
Woman:	They're here, in my handbag. And we checked in online before we left so there are no tickets to worry about. It's the guidebooks. I was planning to bring a couple, so I could do some reading on the journey. I'm pretty sure I didn't pack them, so they're probably still sitting on my desk.
Narrator:	Now listen again.

Narrator: **5 What will the weather be like when the plane arrives?**

Woman: Good morning, everyone. This is your captain speaking. We're currently flying at around ten thousand metres and travelling at 650 kilometres per hour. There's hardly any cloud around and the air is nice and calm. So, the rest of the flight should be smooth and much better than the rather windy day we left behind in London. There's a little light rain in Madrid at the moment, but you'll be pleased to know that it should be clear by the time we arrive in about an hour.

Narrator: Now listen again.

Narrator: **6 What was damaged during the journey?**

Woman: How was your journey?

Man: Well, the ferry was delayed but there's a good shop next to the harbour, so I bought myself a new travel bag. I didn't realize at the time but it's torn at one end so I'll have to return it. Fortunately I haven't put anything in it.

Woman: Oh, dear. How was the sea?

Man: It was really windy, so the boat was moving all over the place! The lady next to me spilled coffee over some documents she had – and I dropped my tablet. Fortunately it didn't break.

Narrator: Now listen again.

Narrator: **7 Where can you park your car for free?**

Man: This is an announcement for the person who has left a car outside the main entrance to the building. The number is AC 4124. Please return to your car and remove the vehicle immediately as parking is not allowed there. There are spaces available in the car park next to the station building where there is no charge. If there are no spaces left, please park on the road at the front of the station. Please note that there is a fee for parking there. Thank you.

Narrator: Now listen again.

3 1 b   2 d   3 a   4 f   5 c   6 e

Listening Part 1:3

1 1 waterfall   4 cliff   7 rainforest
   2 coast   5 valley   8 cave
   3 ocean   6 continent

2 1 heavily   4 loudly
   2 softly   5 lightly
   3 beautifully   6 quietly

3 1 C   2 C   3 A   4 A
   5 B   6 C   7 A

Narrator: 🔊 **Track 3 Listening Part 1 Worksheet 3**

There are seven questions in this part. For each question there are three pictures and a short recording. For each question, choose the correct answer (A, B or C).

Narrator: **1 Which is the girl's favourite photo?**

Girl: Hi, Dad.

Man: Hi. You've been out a long time with your granddad.

Girl: I know. We went for a drive. I took some photos on my new phone – it's got an amazing camera.

Man: So a good day then! I remember those pictures you took looking up at the cliffs from the beach! And that great one of Sam climbing on the rocks.

Girl: Well, I've taken some even better ones today. We stopped at this waterfall which was really high. You can even go behind it – so I did and I got a brilliant picture of it. It's the best one I've taken for ages. Look!

Narrator: Now listen again.

Narrator: **2 What should people not do?**

Woman: Here we are in the national park. I must ask you to stay on the paths – there are rare plants here, and we don't want anyone to stand on them. Take your time and walk slowly so you can look at everything. There's a stream down to the right of the path, but there's a steep drop and the bridge below isn't safe, so don't go down there. We'll get a chance to walk along and even through the river later. We'll also be visiting some caves this afternoon.

Narrator: Now listen again.

Narrator: **3 What has the woman studied in college this week?**

Man: Are you enjoying your geography course at college?

Woman:	Yeah – I've found out all kinds of interesting things. Last month we studied deserts. Did you know there are different types? Some are rock and some are sand. But now we're doing all about the coast. This week we're studying beaches. Today, we went on a trip to a beach with cool patterns in the sand. I really enjoyed it but last week's was really interesting. We studied plants that live near the sea. Did you know some trees like to grow in sand?
Narrator:	Now listen again.
Narrator:	**4 Where does the man prefer to swim?**
Woman:	You swim a lot, don't you, Tim?
Man:	Yeah – I really enjoy swimming outside rather than in indoor pools. The water's cooler and fresher. I especially like moving water like you get in rivers, but you have to be careful. However, there aren't any good swimming rivers near here, so I usually go to the lake. We're a long way from the sea here, so I haven't any experience of swimming there, but I'm looking forward to giving it a try.
Narrator:	Now listen again.
Woman:	**5 What did the students enjoy learning about in the lecture today?**
Man:	What did you think of the lecture this afternoon?
Woman:	Well, I never expected to study anything about farming because we've done so much about natural landscapes, you know, ones that humans *haven't* created.
Man:	It was just as good as studying the rainforest and stuff like that, though, wasn't it?
Woman:	Yeah, I think I preferred it. It was easier to understand.
Man:	I think we're going to be studying the sea next. I guess that'll be good, too. We're going to look at how bays and cliffs are created I think.
Narrator:	Now listen again.
Narrator:	**6 How did the family travel in Iceland?**
Boy:	How was your family trip to Iceland?
Girl:	Brilliant!
Boy:	What did you see?

Girl:	The scenery was amazing – there are hardly any trees there and a lot of strange rock shapes… .You can go around the island by bus with a tour guide. But my dad was brave and decided to hire a car, so we went around in that. We could get really close to nature that way. One day we picked up some walkers and took them back to their hotel. They were really tired but told us some great stories about how the land was created.
Narrator:	Now listen again.
Narrator:	**7 What did the friends learn about in the TV programme?**
Woman:	I watched an interesting programme about the weather last night.
Man:	Oh, yeah, I saw that too. When it started it showed lots of pictures of clouds, didn't it? So, I thought it was going to be about rain and snow and stuff.
Woman:	Yeah – but it actually looked at wind, didn't it – and how it gets stronger and weaker and everything as it travels.
Man:	Mmm, I liked the bit about sea breezes and why it's cooler on the coast even on a hot, sunny day.
Narrator:	Now listen again.

Get it right!
It's **much bigger** than the old wardrobe.

Listening Part 2:1

1a
annoyed – angry	miserable – unhappy
awful – terrible	nervous – anxious
challenging – difficult	relaxed – calm
funny – amusing	strange – unusual
intelligent – clever	surprised – amazed

1b 1 surprised / amazed
2 challenging / difficult

2 1 C   2 B   3 C   4 B   5 A   6 C

Narrator:	🔊 **Track 4 Listening Part 2 Worksheet 1**
	You will hear an interview with a TV actress called Brittany Briers. For each question, choose the correct answer A, B or C.
Man:	We've got TV actress Brittany Briers in the studio. Brittany, how did you discover your love of acting?

Brittany: When I was twelve, Mum sent me to drama classes – I was always trying to be like TV characters at home, though I never thought that was acting. The others in the class were more experienced and that made me nervous, but I learned enough to act in a school play. Being on stage then was definitely what got me interested!

Man: What was your first professional theatre performance like?

Brittany: You'll probably expect me to say I felt calm 'cos of my training. The opposite was true! The person I played had an American accent – I kept thinking I'd go back to my own. I'm sure things like not remembering your lines are embarrassing when there's a huge audience. I made sure that didn't happen.

Man: Later you went into TV acting. Why?

Brittany: It wasn't that I got bored of the theatre. I was seen on stage by a director who thought I was perfect for a TV series he was making. I thought 'Why not learn some fresh skills?' The extra money was useful 'cos I was saving for a house – I'd never take a job just for money though.

Man: Is TV filming more difficult than stage acting?

Brittany: It's different. There's no audience, no clapping. That's strange at first, though the director will tell you when you've done well. Sometimes you film the same bit over and over. That's annoying till you realize it's important to get it right. Then, in a theatre you have to make sure people at the back can hear – on screen that sounds like shouting. I have to be reminded about that lots!

Man: What do you love most about your job?

Brittany: When a new TV series comes out and my family get excited – I prefer not to watch myself on screen and I've never been to any actors' events – though I wouldn't mind doing that one day. I get the real excitement from picking up the envelope containing my next role and I start reading the lines straight away.

Man: Is there anything you don't like about being an actor?

Brittany: Some people find it hard to deal with being recognized in the street. That isn't my favourite part of the job but I accept it – most people are friendly. Getting up before it's light is something I've never got used to, and I never will! But once a series is finished, you can take a long break if you need to.

Narrator: Now listen again.

3 1 boring   4 amazing
   2 confused   5 interesting
   3 disappointed   6 excited

Listening Part 2:2

1 1 went   4 use to watch
   2 used to get up / got up   5 passed
   3 used to work   6 used to close

2 1 B   2 A   3 C   4 C   5 A   6 B

Narrator: 🔊 **Track 5 Listening Part 2 Worksheet 2**

You will hear an interview in which a businesswoman called Carla Smith is talking about her life and work. For each question, choose the correct answer, A, B or C.

Man: This morning we're talking to businesswoman Carla Smith, who's made some changes to the way she lives her life. Carla, the first thing you did was change the way you worked. Why?

Carla: I used to have a busy job – I worked for a large technology firm. It was interesting, so I never got stressed or needed time off like some of my colleagues, who became ill. The job was incredible. I travelled all over the world. Then, suddenly I realized I was living in hotels and I thought 'You know what? I'd like to spend more time in my own house!'

Man: And now you run your own business.

Carla: Yes, and I choose which hours I work. I still do long days – but I can stop when I want to. I didn't use to go on holidays often and I still don't – but that's my choice instead of my company's. Some people who leave big companies miss the big salaries, but that doesn't bother me.

Man: Do you do more exercise now?

Carla:	I spend about the same amount of time exercising as I did before. However, instead of doing it between work and dinner, I get up at 5 am and exercise then. I'm into yoga, I have been for years, because it relaxes my body *and* mind. I've never really enjoyed team sports or athletics.
Man:	What about food? Are you healthier now?
Carla:	Definitely! I never used to have lunch and I ended up eating late and having too much chocolate and crisps, which made me feel bad. Now I cook everything from fresh and it tastes so much nicer. I'm less tired now and have loads of energy – which was unexpected!
Man:	Do you spend more time with family now, too?
Carla:	Yes, particularly my sisters. We've always loved films – when we were teenagers we used to go to the cinema every week. That isn't always possible now, so we have film nights at my house instead. There's an outdoor pool in town and you can swim and watch films there – we're going to try that soon.
Man:	You're still a busy person – do you have any time-saving advice?
Carla:	There are things people do like checking emails or messages on the bus to work or school and making a list of things to do the next day, which are good ideas and can sometimes save time. But the thing that works well for me is having lots of clothes which are the same, so you don't have to think about what to put on in the morning!
Narrator:	Now listen again.

3a 1 I always used to be late for college.
    2 Zijin didn't use to exercise at all.
    3 My son didn't use to get up early as a teenager. / As a teenager my son didn't use to get up early.
    4 Stephanie never used to eat vegetables.
    5 You used to reply to emails immediately.
    6 Ahmed used to drink a lot of coffee.

3b 1 e   2 c   3 f   4 a   5 d   6 b

Listening Part 2:3

1 1 traffic lights   4 tourist information centre
    2 underground train   5 apartment block / building
    3 public transport   6 city centre

2 1 C   2 A   3 B   4 C   5 A   6 B

Narrator:	🔊 **Track 6 Listening Part 2 Worksheet 3**
	You will hear an interview with an architect called Scott Tenbury. For each question, choose the correct answer, A, B or C.
Woman:	Scott Tenbury, you're an architect and you've lived in some interesting buildings for research. Tell us about the one in Japan.
Scott:	I had what's called a 'capsule' in an apartment block. It was one tiny room – I had to be creative and use interesting ways of getting everything I needed into the space. People asked 'Isn't it a bit like living in prison?' But it's nothing like that! And I never heard the neighbours, despite living so close to them.
Woman:	Interesting! You also once lived in what you called an 'upside-down' house.
Scott:	That's right. It looked like the roof was on the ground and the front door was in the air! All the rooms were in their usual place inside, so it wasn't that different to live in it. That was a bit disappointing. It wasn't in an area that tourists visit, but I used to see people taking photos of it from time to time. They'd ask whether the house was difficult to look after – it wasn't at all.
Woman:	You've also lived in a container in London – one of those big metal boxes which ships carry things in.
Scott:	Yes – in the city centre. Unfortunately, it had a metal roof and when it rained, I couldn't hear the television! I wasn't sorry to leave that behind when I sold it. It took me a while to sell it – although they're small, they're not cheap, but I managed to sell it to a young woman – she was an architect too.
Woman:	Have you always lived in cities?
Scott:	Yes, they're wonderful. It's great watching all those people living their lives – doing similar things in different ways! Many people like going to restaurants, shopping centres – I'm not bothered about all that. I work from home, so could live anywhere, but I love cities.
Woman:	What are you designing at the moment?

Scott:	I'm working on my 'water building', trying to make a box which appears to float on the water – that's going well. People have been building on water for centuries, so there are no difficulties there. I want it to be the same grey-blue as the water – it seems almost impossible, because water changes so much with the light!
Woman:	What kind of building would you like to design?
Scott:	A railway station – one that's on different levels. A big monument to trains! It's not because I want people to say 'Wow!' but I'd like the challenge of making something so big and that does something useful but is beautiful to look at, too.
Narrator:	Now listen again.

3 1 <u>un</u>forgettable   5 depart<u>ment</u>
    2 danger<u>ous</u>   6 <u>im</u>possible
    3 wonder<u>ful</u>   7 inform<u>ation</u>
    4 <u>dis</u>advantage   8 friend<u>ship</u>

Get it right!
I remember the beautiful beaches where we **used to** play volleyball.

Listening Part 3:1

1 1 How often do you go to the cinema?
    2 Have you ever been to a music festival?
    3 Do you enjoy reading?
    4 Did you do any exercise last weekend?
    5 Can you play a musical instrument?
    6 Are you a gamer?

2 1 cartoon   3 lake   5 restaurant
    2 chef   4 movies   6 January 28th

Narrator:	🔊 **Track 7 Listening Part 3 Worksheet 1**
	You will hear a film review programme on the radio.
	For each question, fill in the missing information in the numbered space.
Man:	Welcome to The Film Review Programme! Today we're reviewing some of this week's new films.
	Let's start with this week's likely hit, *Jungle Fever*. This is quite an unusual one! Some of you may remember last year's TV documentary film about a family of tigers in India. Well, this is a cartoon based on that programme and I can report that it's great fun for people of any age.

Some of you will be excited to know that actor Steve Wills is back on our screens! You'll remember him as action hero Marty Kay, but in his new film, *Call it*, he actually plays a chef, working in an Italian pizza takeaway in New York City. Actor Jennifer Peckory plays his manager, Jo-Jo, and romance is in the air!

Don't miss *Swim!*, a comedy which takes a look at learning to swim as an adult. It's about a 20-year-old man who wants to join in with his friends when they swim in the lake near his home. So, he goes to the local pool to take lessons. Be prepared to laugh until it hurts!

And now it's competition time, so I hope you've listened carefully and made some notes! If you want to enter this month's competition, just go online and answer the ten questions in our quiz. Go to www dot movies dot co and select your answers.

Last month, we gave out free cinema tickets as a prize – this time we're offering restaurant tickets which you can use at a choice of exciting places.

You must complete your entry by January the twenty-eighth. Make sure you've finished by two pm when the competition closes. We'll announce the winners on the thirtieth of January – and if you're lucky, the prize will be yours by the second week in February. Good luck and goodbye!

Narrator:	Now listen again.

3 1 d   2 b   3 e   4 f   5 c   6 a

Listening Part 3:2

1 1 buy   4 stores
    2 displays   5 alone
    3 spend   6 gifts

2 1 have / get; cut   4 had / got; painted
    2 have / get; repaired   5 had / got; repaired
    3 has / gets; delivered   6 have / get; washed

3 1 Hickets
    2 ground
    3 Thursday
    4 bus
    5 food
    6 ID card

Narrator: **Track 8 Listening Part 3 Worksheet 2**

You will hear part of a training session for people who are going to work as sales assistants in a large shop. For each question, fill in the missing information in the numbered space.

Mandy: Morning, everyone! Thanks for attending this training session at our new department store. You've all been offered jobs as sales assistants, so well done and welcome! My name's Mandy Hickets – that's H-I-C-K-E-T-S – and I'm your training manager.

I'll tell you a bit about how the store's organized. The top floor's where the stock room is – that's where everything's kept before it goes out onto the shelves. The first floor's mainly clothing, and the ground floor, where you'll work, is where we sell things like make-up and electrical items.

Most of you are part-time staff, which means you'll work from Monday to Saturday, either in the mornings or the afternoons. Your rest day is Thursday. Full-time staff take either a Tuesday or a Wednesday off – you'll find out which later today.

I know that some of you live out of town. There's a regular train service as I'm sure you already know, but we also operate a bus service for those nearer by. There's no charge for this. There's also a staff car park, though you'll need to pay a small monthly fee for this.

All staff get 25% discount on certain items and services. You could have your hair cut in our salon, for example, and you can use the discount when the sales are on, too, which some stores don't offer. I'm afraid there are no discounts on food, however.

I believe you've already ordered your uniforms and you'll be able to collect those at the end of today's session. When you arrive on your first day, please go to the office, where you'll pick up your ID card. We provide keys for lockers, where you can keep your personal items safe. These are already in the locker doors, ready for use.

Let's get on with the training. Now ....

Narrator: Now listen again.

Listening Part 3:3

1
1 chin
2 ankle
3 heel
4 thumb
5 knee
6 shoulder

2
1 army
2 bridge
3 jogging
4 trainers
5 30th September [and all possible written alternatives]
6 Shawes

Narrator: **Track 9 Listening Part 3 Worksheet 3**

You will hear a talk about an exercise class called Extreme Bootcamp. For each question, fill in the missing information in the numbered space.

Woman: Hi, everyone. I'd like to tell you about a new exercise class I've just tried. It's called 'Extreme Bootcamp' and it's hard but great fun!

What does 'bootcamp' mean? It's actually a word used by the army when they're training new soldiers. It's nothing to do with what's on your feet. And believe me, it's nothing like a camping trip either! It's a short course of challenging physical training.

Most of us are used to exercising in the gym, with nothing but TV screens or other people to look at while we're on the machines or whatever. But Extreme Bootcamp is different 'cos you do the class on a bridge. It goes over a river, so it's nice to look at while you exercise.

You won't like the sound of this, but the class meets at 6.30 am every weekday for a month. It's only for an hour but class members do lots in that time, beginning with jogging to warm up. After that there's some weight lifting and jumping, and then you do some more relaxing exercises at the end.

The clothes you should wear are pretty much the same as you'd wear for any other exercise class – so a T-shirt and shorts or a tracksuit is fine. Oh, and wearing trainers is a must, so do bring a good pair with you.

Bootcamp is good fun, I promise! If you're interested in joining the next one, there's a registration day on 17th September – though the first class won't be until the 30th.

The bootcamp's run by Ellie Shawes and she can give you more information if you need it. Her surname's spelt S-H-A-W-E-S, and you can contact her via the website. I've got her phone number too if you want it. OK, so has anyone got any questions?

Narrator: Now listen again.

3a
1 to take	4 resting
2 visiting	5 to get
3 seeing	6 to pick up

3b Students' own answers

Get it right!

I will spend a few days **going** shopping.

Listening Part 4:1

1
1 are collected	4 was recycled
2 is; picked up	5 is caused
3 was predicted	6 were bought

2 1 A   2 A   3 B   4 A   5 B   6 A

Narrator: 🔊 **Track 10 Listening Part 4 Worksheet 1**

Look at the six sentences for this part. You will hear two local politicians, a man called Robin and a woman called Lisa, talking about recycling in their town. Decide if each sentence is correct or incorrect. If it is correct, put a tick in the box under A for YES. If it is not correct, put a tick in the box under B for NO.

Lisa: Right, we need to look at the facts and figures about our town's recycling efforts this year.

Robin: I guess we've still got a long way to go before we reach our goal of 50 per cent recycling of waste collected from people's homes.

Lisa: Actually, we aren't as far away from what we want to achieve as that. I believe we're already managing to recycle about 45 per cent.

Robin: That's better than I expected. So, shall we start with metal? We're doing OK – a large number of cans are recycled each year, but we could encourage people to do more. They can be recycled quickly and they're ready to use again in six weeks.

Lisa: It's a pity the companies which recycle them can't do it in half the time.

Robin: I know.

Lisa: How about progress on the recycling of glass? I think we could improve on that, too. There aren't enough bins for people to take their empty bottles to.

Robin: Well, it's all about money, isn't it? New bins aren't cheap. Moving on… Let's look at the recycling of paper. The town's doing pretty well on that. The average person uses 38 kilos of newspaper every year – and we're recycling over half of it.

Lisa: Really? That's an improvement on last year. Now, plastic. That's a different story. People are throwing too much away.

Robin: It isn't that there's no information about how dangerous plastic is to the environment – there's plenty! Maybe we should think about introducing fines for people who put it in ordinary bins instead of recycling ones.

Lisa: That's not a bad idea. Shall we finish with traffic? We've managed to cut air pollution by promoting the car share plan. More people are travelling together to work.

Robin: That's good, but I thought we were trying to reduce fares. They're still too high, which is a shame. We need to encourage more people to use our new, cleaner buses!

Narrator: Now listen again.

3a
1 borrow	4 take	7 teach
2 do	5 Tell	8 miss
3 wasting	6 met	

3b Students' own answers

Listening Part 4:2

1
1 chatting	4 post	7 sharing
2 download	5 update	8 blog
3 upload	6 podcasts	

2 1 B   2 B   3 A   4 A   5 A   6 B

Narrator: 🔊 **Track 11 Listening Part 4 Worksheet 2**

Look at the six sentences for this part. You will hear a young woman called Sylvia and a man called Ted talking about using social media. Decide if each sentence is correct or incorrect. If it is correct, put a tick in the box under A for YES. If it is not correct, put a tick in the box under B for NO.

Sylvia:	How much time do you spend on social media every day?
Ted:	It depends. I spend a lot of time on Instagram – people post some incredible pictures on there… I can browse for hours without realizing. I don't feel guilty – it's pretty useful for the work I do on the school magazine.
Sylvia:	Oh, yeah, I guess it would be. I'd say I'm connected to social media all the time I'm awake, unless I'm doing my homework… I've got to admit that I leave my mobile on when I'm in bed – and if it pings I'll pick it up!
Ted:	I'm not shocked 'cos I've noticed how you always answer texts immediately! Doesn't it keep you awake? I've read that looking at screens like that at night – all that blue light – makes it difficult to sleep.
Sylvia:	Well, that's true I'm afraid. I should probably stop looking at stuff just before I go to bed.
Ted:	Do you use Snapchat to send photos and videos? I get some amazing stuff sent to me. I wish it didn't disappear again so quickly!
Sylvia:	Yeah – they get deleted in a few seconds after you've seen them. I do have a few laughs with friends using it – but I don't want to spend all my time using it.
Ted:	What about Facebook? You know what I get tired of? People going on about how exciting their lives are – though I'm sure they're not that brilliant really!
Sylvia:	It's not what it was invented for, is it? Really it was for connecting people – chatting to friends who might live on the other side of the world. Change is a positive thing, though, so people should do what they want with it.
Ted:	You're right… Oh, I'm following you on Twitter now!
Sylvia:	I invited you ages ago!
Ted:	I know. It's just not my thing. I'm not that bothered about knowing what someone's doing every minute of every day.
Sylvia:	I find myself reading stuff for hours – when I should be doing other things – plus, it's a good way to learn.
Ted:	I'm sure you're right.
Narrator:	Now listen again.

3a
1 although
2 before
3 plus
4 Since
5 Unless
6 While

3b Students' own answers

Listening Part 4:3

1
1 Portuguese
2 Spain
3 Chinese
4 Turkish
5 Russia
6 French
7 Italy

2 1 A 2 B 3 A 4 B 5 A 6 A

Narrator:	🔊 **Track 12 Listening Part 4 Worksheet 3**
	Look at the six sentences for this part. You will hear a man called Aaron and a woman called Sophia talking about learning languages. Decide if each sentence is correct or incorrect. If it is correct, put a tick in the box under A for YES. If it is not correct, put a tick in the box under B for NO.
Aaron:	That was a great Japanese lesson today.
Sophia:	Yeah, I enjoy trying to write the characters – though I haven't found a system for remembering them yet. It's challenging studying a language that's so different from your own, isn't it?
Aaron:	You need a bit of brain power sometimes, yeah. Personally, I don't think I'll ever speak any language other than English perfectly. But so many people speak English around the world that it doesn't matter if you can't speak anything else.
Sophia:	I think being able to use at least a few words when you travel abroad is a really positive thing to do! It helps you create better relationships with people from other countries.
Aaron:	Well, I learn languages because I enjoy doing it. I don't really travel a lot.
Sophia:	Anyway, you've got a much better memory than I have for learning new words – how do you do that?
Aaron:	I don't know – it just seems to happen! I don't make a lot of effort to remember things, they just seem to stay in my head.
Sophia:	Lucky you. You know what I love most about learning languages?
Aaron:	Go on.

Sophia:	When someone who speaks the language you're learning actually understands what you're saying in it! Of course, I don't always get what they're saying back to me, but never mind. You can ask people to repeat what they've said – or use a dictionary to help.
Aaron:	I don't seem to have too many problems with listening… I'd say speaking's probably my strongest skill – but putting things down on paper is where I have most problems. It helps if you read a lot, though, then you know how things are spelled, that kind of thing.
Sophia:	I know. I don't think getting things wrong is actually something we should try to avoid – that's the way you learn.
Aaron:	'Cos you're more likely to remember something if someone has to correct you? Yeah – I'd agree with you there.
Narrator:	Now listen again.

3 1 ✗ which/that   4 ✓
   2 ✓   5 ✗ Whose
   3 ✓   6 ✗ who / that

Get it right!

This party **was** organised by my old school friend.

Speaking Part 1:1

1 1 What's your name?
   2 How do you spell your surname?
   3 Where do you come from?
   4 Do you study English at college?
   5 Where do you live?

2a 1 spend   4 would   7 live
    2 enjoy   5 start   8 had
    3 like   6 grow

Narrator: **Track 13 Speaking Part 1 Worksheet 1**

1 Who do you spend most time with?
2 What do you enjoy doing when you're at home?
3 What do you like about your school or job?
4 What would you like to do in the future?
5 When did you start learning English? Do you enjoy it? Why? / Why not?
6 Where did you grow up?
7 What do you like about the town you live in?
8 Where would you like to live, if you had the opportunity?

---

3 1 cousin   3 couple   5 anniversary
   2 married   4 generations 6 nephew

Speaking Part 1:2

1 1 d   2 c   3 g   4 a
   5 f   6 e   7 h   8 b

2a 1 work   5 difficult
    2 school   6 outside
    3 favourite   7 job
    4 subject   8 ambition

Narrator: **Track 14 Speaking Part 1 Worksheet 2**

1 Do you study or work? What are you studying? / What do you do?
2 Do you like your school or job? Why? Why not?
3 What is or was your favourite subject at school? What do or did you like most about it?
4 Which subject would you like to learn more about?
5 What do you find difficult about learning English?
6 How often do you use English outside of your English classes?
7 If you could have any job, what would you do and why?
8 What is your greatest study or work ambition?

---

3 1 could / was able to   4 been able to
   2 can   5 can't
   3 will be able to   6 couldn't

Speaking Part 1:3

1a 1 d   2 e   3 b   4 c   5 f   6 a

1b Students' own answers

2a 1 free time   5 country
    2 sports   6 activities
    3 take part   7 extreme
    4 doing   8 weekend

Narrator: **Track 15 Speaking Part 1 Worksheet 3**

1 What do you enjoy doing in your free time?
2 Do you enjoy playing sports? Which ones?
3 Do you prefer to watch sports rather than take part in them?

---

4 Do you enjoy doing things with other people?
5 What are the most popular sports or hobbies in your country?
6 What activities would you most like to try?
7 Have you ever tried any extreme sports? Did you enjoy it?
8 How did you spend last weekend?

3
1	At first	3	so	5	what's more
2	Anyway	4	While	6	After

Get it right!
But it would be better if you **could** take part, too.

Speaking Part 2:1

1
1	should	5	because / as / since
2	because / as / since	6	would
3	don't	7	so
4	could / (should)	8	as / since

2a a makes   b Let's

2b
1 The traffic jam made me late for the concert.
2 Let's go to that new bookshop in town this afternoon.
3 Let's go to see the new James Bond film. / Let's go to the new James Bond film.
4 Our basketball coach made us run 5 km.

3
> **Narrator:** **Track 16 Speaking Part 2 Worksheet 1**
>
> A girl is having her **sixteenth birthday party** next week. Her friends want to buy her a present, but they don't have much **money**. Talk together about the different presents they could give her and say which would be **best**.
>
> Here is a picture with some ideas to help you.

Speaking Part 2:2

1
1	shall	3	would	5	have
2	about	4	don't	6	fancy

2 Example answers
1 Have you got a table (for two), please?
2 Could I / we see the menu, please?
3 Yes, please. I'll have / I'd like a lemonade and my friend will have / would like a coffee.
4 I'll have / I'd like the chicken salad and my friend will have / would like a pizza.
5 Yes, thank you. / It's delicious! / I'm afraid the soup is a little cold / too spicy. / There's too much salt in the soup.
6 No, thank you. Can I / we have the bill, please?
7 By credit card, please. / I'll / we'll pay in cash.

3
> **Narrator:** **Track 17 Speaking Part 2 Worksheet 2**
>
> A group of students is having a **party** to celebrate the end of the school year. Each student has to bring some **food**. Talk together about the different **types** of food the students could bring and say which would be **best** for a class party.
>
> Here is a picture with some ideas to help you.

Speaking Part 2:3

1 Example answers
1 I guess that some people don't worry about danger.
2 To be honest, I don't like dancing.
3 I have no doubt that active people are healthier.
4 I agree that it's best to do something different, but there isn't always time.
5 I feel that spending times with my friends is really important.
6 Personally, I find doing nothing really hard.
7 I don't think that they are a waste of time. You can learn things from TV.

2
1	too	4	enough
2	such	5	so
3	so	6	too

3
> **Narrator:** **Track 18 Speaking Part 2 Worksheet 3**
>
> Two friends are going away for a **weekend**. Their parents will pay for them to do an **exciting new activity**. Talk together about the different activities they could do and say which would be most exciting to try for the **first time**.
>
> Here is a picture with some ideas to help you.

Get it right!
They are such pleasant people.

Speaking Part 3 / 4:1

1
1	along / down / on	5	on
2	the middle	6	straight
3	in front / ahead	7	Behind
4	between	8	in

2
1 b	2 d	3 a	4 c	5 f	6 e

3
> **Narrator:** **Track 19 Speaking Parts 3 and 4 Worksheet 1**
>
> Now, I'd like each of you to talk on your own about something. I'm going to give each of you a photograph of people who are travelling. Candidate A, here is your photograph (photograph 1).

Please show it to Candidate B, but I'd like you to talk about it. Candidate B, you just listen. I'll give you your photograph in a moment. Candidate A, please tell us what you can see in the photograph.

Now, Candidate B, here is your photograph (photograph 2). It also shows people who are travelling. Please show it to Candidate A and tell us what you can see in the photograph.

4

> **Narrator:** **Track 20 Speaking Parts 3 and 4 Worksheet 1**
>
> Your photographs showed people and transport. Now, I'd like you to talk together about the advantages and disadvantages of travelling by bus or by train, and which form of public transport you like using most.

Speaking Part 3 / 4:2

1 Example answers
  a It looks like a pair of sunglasses.
  b It might be a flip flop / sandal.
  c It looks like a travel plug / an adaptor.
  d It seems to be a passport.
  e It looks as if it's a boarding pass.
  f It could be headphones / an MP3 player.

2 Example answers
  1 No way! / That's amazing! / Wow!
  2 Did you? / Oh really? / Wow!
  3 Do they! / Oh really? / Oh yeah!
  4 Are you? / That's amazing! / Oh really? / Wow!
  5 Oh really? / Oh yeah? / That's interesting.
  6 Oh really? / Oh yeah? / Is he?
  7 Did you? / Oh really? / That's a pity!
  8 Wow! / That's amazing. / Did she?

3

> **Narrator:** **Track 21 Speaking Parts 3 and 4 Worksheet 2**
>
> Now, I'd like each of you to talk on your own about something. I'm going to give each of you a photograph of people on holiday.
>
> Candidate A, here is your photograph (photograph 1). Please show it to Candidate B, but I'd like you to talk about it. Candidate B, you just listen. I'll give you your photograph in a moment.
>
> Candidate A, please tell us what you can see in the photograph.
>
> Now, Candidate B, here is your photograph (photograph 2). It also shows people on holiday. Please show it to Candidate A and tell us what you can see in the photograph.

4

> **Narrator:** **Track 22 Speaking Parts 3 and 4 Worksheet 2**
>
> Your photographs showed people on holiday. Now, I'd like you to talk together about the kinds of holidays you like and the best holiday you have ever had.

Speaking Part 3 / 4:3

1 a gate   f mirror
  b garage   g cooker
  c balcony   h stairs
  d bookcase   i lamp
  e basin

2 1 d   2 a   3 c   4 f
  5 e   6 g   7 h   8 b

3

> **Narrator:** **Track 23 Speaking Parts 3 and 4 Worksheet 3**
>
> Now, I'd like each of you to talk on your own about something. I'm going to give each of you a photograph of people spending time at home.
>
> Candidate A, here is your photograph (photograph 1). Please show it to Candidate B, but I'd like you to talk about it. Candidate B, you just listen. I'll give you your photograph in a moment.
>
> Candidate A, please tell us what you can see in the photograph.
>
> Now, Candidate B, here is your photograph (photograph 2). It also shows people spending time at home. Please show it to Candidate A and tell us what you can see in the photograph.

4

> **Narrator:** **Track 24 Speaking Parts 3 and 4 Worksheet 3**
>
> Your photographs showed people spending time at home. Now, I'd like you to talk together about how you spend time at home, and what you do when relatives or friends come to visit.

Get it right!
I didn't know that this city **could** be so interesting.
It **would** be nice to see *The Merchant of Venice* with Al Pacino.

Think about it

Preliminary Reading Part 1

1	True	5	True
2	False	6	False
3	True	7	True
4	True	8	True

Preliminary Reading Part 2

1	match	5	points
2	five	6	suitable
3	eight	7	text
4	people	8	all

Preliminary Reading Part 3

1	longer	5	don't have to
2	might be some	6	A; B
3	ten	7	follows
4	detailed	8	before

Preliminary Reading Part 4

1	five	5	global
2	four	6	detailed
3	opinion	7	order
4	purpose	8	first

Preliminary Reading Part 5

False sentences: 3, 7

Preliminary Writing Part 1

1 True
2 False. The sentences have a common topic.
3 True
4 True
5 False. You must use one to three words.
6 True
7 True
8 True

Preliminary Writing Part 2

1	short	5	don't have to
2	tells	6	35
3	three	7	45
4	must	8	lower

Preliminary Writing Part 3

1	choose	4	reply
2	story	5	title
3	100	6	topic

7	imagination	10	middle
8	organise	11	vocabulary
9	start	12	mistakes

Preliminary Listening Part 1

1	recordings	5	people
2	multiple-choice	6	vocabulary
3	pictures	7	mark
4	facts		

Preliminary Listening Part 2

1	True	5	True
2	False	6	False
3	False	7	False
4	True		

Preliminary Listening Part 3

1	False	5	True
2	True	6	False; False
3	True	7	False
4	True		

Preliminary Listening Part 4

1	e	5	c
2	a	6	d
3	f	7	h
4	b	8	g

Preliminary Speaking Part 1

1	False	5	False
2	False	6	True
3	True	7	True
4	True	8	True

Preliminary Speaking Part 2

1	situation	5	opinions
2	partner	6	interested
3	pictures	7	opportunity
4	instructions	8	stop

Preliminary Speaking Part 3

1	e	3	a	5	b	7	h
2	g	4	d	6	c	8	f

Preliminary Speaking Part 4

1	a	3	a	5	b	7	a
2	b	4	a	6	b	8	b

ACKNOWLEDGEMENTS

Development of this publication has made use of the Cambridge English Corpus, a multi-billion word collection of spoken and written English. It includes the Cambridge Learner Corpus, a unique collection of candidate exam answers. Cambridge University Press has built up the Cambridge English Corpus to provide evidence about language use that helps to produce better language teaching materials.

The authors and publishers acknowledge the following sources of copyright material and are grateful for the permissions granted. While every effort has been made, it has not always been possible to identify the sources of all the material used, or to trace all copyright holders. If any omissions are brought to our notice, we will be happy to include the appropriate acknowledgements on reprinting and in the next update to the digital edition, as applicable.

Key: TL = Top Left, TR = Top Right, BR = Below Right.

p. 6: ScottTalent/DigitalVision Vectors/Getty Images; p. 8: David Lees/Taxi/Getty Images; p. 9: zacky24/iStock/Getty Images; p. 10: Paolo Cordelli/Lonely Planet Images/Getty Images; p. 12 (Photo 1): Michael Blann/Stone/Getty Images; p. 12 (Photo 2): Neil Beckerman/Taxi/Getty Images; p. 12 (Photo 3): Design Pics/Getty Images; p. 12 (Photo 4): Dave and Les Jacobs/Kolostock/Blend Images/ Getty Images; p. 12 (Photo 5): Ogphoto/E+/Getty Images; p. 14 (Photo 1): Vesna Andjic/E+/Getty Images; p. 14 (Photo 2): moodboard/Brand X Pictures/Getty Images; p. 14 (Photo 3): David Schaffer/ Caiaimage/Getty Images; p. 14 (Photo 4): Justin Case/DigitalVision/Getty Images; p. 14 (Photo 5): Jacqueline Veissid/DigitalVision/Getty Images; p. 16 (Photo 1): Dougal Waters/DigitalVision/Getty Images; p. 16 (Photo 2): Mike Harrington/The Image Bank/Getty Images; p. 16 (Photo 3): Dave and Les Jacobs/Kolostock/Blend Images/Getty Images; p. 16 (Photo 4): Rutherhagen, Peter/Getty Images; p. 16 (Photo 5): Lane Oatey/Blue Jean Images/Getty Images; p. 19: ANDREW YATES/AFP/Getty Images; p. 21 (TR): The Washington Post/Getty Images; p. 21 (BR): UpperCut Images/Getty Images; p. 23: Deb Alperin/Moment/Getty Images; p. 24: Martin Dimitrov/E+/Getty Images; p. 28: monkeybusinessimages/ iStock/Getty Images; p. 30: Isa Foltin/WireImage/Getty Images; p. 32: FRANCOIS GUILLOT/AFP/Getty Images; p. 34: Eastcott Momatiuk/The Image Bank/Getty Images; p. 37: KidStock/Blend Images/Getty Images; p. 38: Robert Daly/OJO Images/Getty Images; p. 41: Marion Nesje/Moment/Getty Images; p. 42: Tom Merton/Caiaimage/Getty Images; p. 45: Lina Arvidsson/Maskot/Getty Images; p. 46: Stephen Simpson/Iconica/Getty Images; p. 50: Steve Sands/Getty Images Entertainment/Getty Images; p. 52: Westend61/Getty Images; p. 60 (Photo 1): Ezra Bailey/Iconica/Getty Images; p. 60 (Photo 2): Ezra Bailey/Iconica/Getty Images; p. 60 (Photo 3): Jekaterina Nikitina/Stone/Getty Images; p. 60 (Photo 4): Flashpop/DigitalVision/Getty Images; p. 62: Jacek Chabraszewski/iStock/Getty Images; p. 65: Dennis Fischer Photography/Moment/Getty Images; p. 66: John Eder/Stone/Getty Images; p. 68: Erik Von Weber/The Image Bank/Getty Images; p. 70: Ryan McVay/DigitalVision/Getty Images; p. 72: Sam Diephuis/Photographer's Choice/Getty Images; p. 75: Westend61/Getty Images; p. 77: TAGSTOCK1/iStock/Getty Images; p. 79: Juanmonino/E+/Getty Images; p. 81: Westend61/Getty Images; p. 82: Poncho/Photolibrary/Getty Images; p. 90: Oli Scarff/Getty Images News/Getty Images; p. 91 (TL): Brent Winebrenner/Lonely Planet Images/Getty Images; p. 91 (TR): Robert Nickelsberg/ Getty Images; p. 92 (Photo a): Tom Fletcher/EyeEm/Getty Images; p. 92 (Photo b): Ursula Alter/ Photographer's Choice/Getty Images; p. 92 (Photo c): Nadine Funke/EyeEm/Getty Images; p. 92 (Photo d): Charlie Drevstam/Getty Images; p. 92 (Photo e): bortonia/DigitalVision Vectors/Getty Images; p. 92 (Photo f): Charlie Abad/Photononstop/Getty Images; p. 93 (TL): Phillip Suddick/Taxi/Getty Images; p. 93 (TR): Rob Stothard/Getty Images News/Getty Images; p. 94: Giordano Poloni/Ikon Images/Getty Images; p. 95 (TL): Hero Images/Getty Images; p. 95 (TR): KidStock/Blend Images/Getty Images.

Illustrations by Daniel Limon

The publishers are grateful to the following contributors:
layout by Q2A Media Services Pvt. Ltd.; audio production by Hart McLeod, Cambridge